GW00706095

THE TEACH YOURSELF BOOKS

UNDERWATER
SWIMMING

**Uniform with this volume
and in the same series**

TEACH YOURSELF
UNDERWATER SWIMMING

Leo Zanelli

THE ENGLISH UNIVERSITIES PRESS LTD
ST. PAUL'S HOUSE WARWICK LANE
LONDON E.C.4

First printed 1967

Copyright © 1967
The English Universities Press Ltd

*Printed in Great Britain
for The English Universities Press Ltd.
by Cox & Wyman, Ltd., Fakenham*

Foreword

The invention of the aqualung by Jacques-Yves Cousteau and Emile Gagnan in 1943 began a new era in underwater exploration and science and for the first time opened the world beneath the seas to the ordinary man and woman. Sub-aqua swimming is now an international recreation and pastime for the very many who find beneath the surface of sea, river and lake a new world—a world of beauty, excitement, and of never-ending interest.

The British Sub-Aqua Club, formed in 1953 from a handful of enthusiasts, has kept pace with—and has helped set the pace for—modern techniques, equipment, and organisation, while the 'handful' of enthusiasts has now reached proportions of many thousands. It is an encouraging aspect of the British diving scene that the majority of divers belong to the B.S-A.C.; for the lone wolf, in any sphere, is seldom in a position to further its cause.

The sea is capable of extracting grave penalties from the untrained. Note that I say untrained, not inexperienced, for even an experienced underwater swimmer can make mistakes, possibly fatal, in adverse conditions—if he has not received accurate basic instruction and training. A sport that possesses even the slightest element of danger (and what really worthwhile sport does not?) cannot possess too many textbooks, providing the authors are experienced in administering instruction and have had extensive knowledge and practice of the difficulties involved. Leo Zanelli, with whom I have dived many times, fulfils these conditions, and I am very happy to extend my best wishes for the success of this book.

HAROLD GOULD
Chairman, British Sub-Aqua Club

Contents

x   Contents

I. The Underwater World

Why Dive?

It is understandable why underwater swimming—particularly free-diving on compressed air—attracts an ever-growing band of enthusiasts, for no other sport can offer so many different aspects. Apart from the satisfaction of achieving a certain standard of physical proficiency with training, the underwater world is the only place left where the man-in-the-street can practise exploration: almost any stretch of coastline possesses underwater sites that have never been seen by man. Marine natural history has more mystery and adventure than the land-based science; the free-diver is able to witness scenery and the activities of marine life that the zoologist could only guess about a few short years ago, and much remains to be discovered. Furthermore, the conscientious amateur free-diver is being used with greater frequency by scientists probing the Continental Shelf. What, then, could be more rewarding or satisfying than an activity which allies physical skill with adventure, mystery, the thrill of exploration, and a contribution to man's knowledge of the world?

A window to the world under the sea has been opened up to the public through cinema and television, and through the exploits of Hans Hass, Mike Nelson, and kindred souls. It is a world that most of us, with competent instruction, can visit—a rich experience that will pervade your memory for life.

A Short History

Free-diving is the descriptive word for underwater swimming using breathing apparatus that is independent of surface attachments. It is not a completely authoritative term, for others (namely, self-contained diving apparatus, SCUBA, and aqualung diver) are used in association with the same activity.

The first free-diving apparatus appears to have been designed and used by a W. H. James in 1825. It consisted of a closed tunic with an integral hood of thick leather fitted with a small plate window. The tunic was fastened at the waist and arms by elastic webbing; air was provided by a hollow cylindrical 'belt' of iron that completely surrounded the torso from hips to chest. The air was compressed to approximately thirty atmospheres, and James is reputed to have obtained up to an hour's diving. (Although the depth is not specified, it must have been shallow for a dive of this duration.)

In 1865, Rouquayrol and Denayrouze evolved a regulator that controlled a flow of air from a compressed air tank. This mechanism, in principle and certain details, is identical to the modern demand valve, but the lack of a suitable high-pressure tank rendered the regulator more useful in conjunction with an air supply by surface hose.

In 1878, H. A. Fleuss, in association with Siebe, Gorman and Co., designed the first practical self-contained breathing apparatus embodying air-regenerating devices. This equipment utilized oxygen and a carbon dioxide absorbent, and was the forerunner of the Second World War frogman apparatus. Prior to 1914, R. H. Davis, who entered Siebe, Gorman and Co. in 1882, collaborated with Fleuss in improving the apparatus; this resulted in the very reliable and efficient

'Proto' and 'Salvus' models, forms of which are still in use today.

By 1926, compressed-air cylinders were available that could hold a substantial pressure, and Commander Y. Le Prieur was experimenting with a type of Rouquayrol–Denayrouze apparatus. Although the equipment possessed certain deficiencies, by equipping the diver with fins and mask, Le Prieur managed to get away from the ancient concept of men walking along the sea-bed. He can lay claim to being the originator of the first really free diver—one who could vie with the fish instead of struggling along the bottom with leaden feet.

During the early part of 1943, in the River Marne, Captain Jacques-Yves Cousteau tested a demand valve designed by Emile Gagnan, an industrial gas engineer. The mechanism, in principle, had evolved from the Rouquayrol–Denayrouze regulator of the last century. The Cousteau–Gagnan demand valve was slightly modified after its first test, becoming a model of simplicity and reliability in operation. Commerce was soon geared to the means of production, and the underwater world was thrown open to man.

A Look at the Future

That much of man's future lies under the sea is without doubt. The greater—and lesser—powers are expending vast sums of money on research into various aspects of the underseas.

Off the east coast of Britain, enormous drilling barges are plunging drills through the bed of the North Sea in search of the vast pockets of gas calculated to reside in caverns beneath. Off the west coast of Africa, diamonds are already being gathered in large quantities, while shallow-water dredging for tin is already in operation off Indonesia.

As a source of food, the world is badly organized to benefit fully from the sea's potential; but the era of technology is swiftly changing this aspect. Some scientists envisage underwater farms that will grow and harvest crops of seaweed and other marine plants. It is possible that certain fish could be 'herded' and domesticated; perhaps electric currents or other rays could seal the estuaries of rivers, restricting fish to a specific area. Deep water photographs have shown vast beds of manganese nodules lying on the ocean floor, awaiting the harvester.

If only a few of the forecasts become reality, a new breed will come into being: the aquanauts. Underwater houses will contain oil riggers, farmers, and miners; this is no pipe-dream, for men are already spending weeks researching at depth. By staying down for long periods, the diver could carry out a vast amount of work, and complete underwater villages are envisaged. The working population will commute on little nuclear scooters, tending the plants or mining minerals.

The idea of man residing under the sea is climaxed by Captain Cousteau's forecast of 'Homo Aquaticus', in which surgery—by the insertion of gills, or a regenerating oxygen cartridge installed in the body—will enable man to exist in water for indefinite periods. This theory, startling as it may seem, has already been proved possible: laboratory tests have been made in which animals existed submerged for long periods with their lungs completely filled with water.

Science has now evolved a membrane so thin that it will allow the passage of gases without hindrance, while still remaining completely watertight. In practice, this means that one could exist underwater enclosed in a 'bubble' of skin, for as oxygen dissolved in the water would filter through the membrane, so exhaled air would pass back. Artificial gills—looking somewhat like plastic bags—have already been fashioned from this membrane and attached to breathing tubes. The human guinea-pigs testing this apparatus have used it for periods exceeding an hour, obtaining their oxygen—like the fish—from the surrounding water.

This activity will no doubt duplicate the terrestrial problem of traffic. The bathyscaph has touched bottom, taking photographs and samples at a depth of seven miles. 'Shallow' watersubmersibles, such as Cousteau's diving saucer, 'Denise', can free-range down to 1,000 feet, carrying a diver and passenger, with a cruising time of several hours. 'Deepstar', now in course of construction, will be a three-man submersible; she will be capable of descending to 400 feet, and, later—with modifications—to 1,200 feet. The 'Aluminaut', a submersible over 50 feet long, constructed of aluminium alloy, will range down to 1,500 feet and have a cruising time of over three days.

During the International Geophysical Year, vast areas of the Pacific were charted; detailed study threw further light on such aspects of oceanology as current circulation, the mineral wealth of the sea-bed, life cycles and population of the flora and fauna, and the mystery of certain rises and falls in sea level.

Facilities for underwater swimmers, in the form of equipment hire, cylinder charging, and tuition, are springing up all over the world—especially at holiday resorts. Organized bodies such as the British Sub-Aqua Club are making great strides in the fields of instruction, training, and diving qualifications. Indeed, Britain has probably the world's first National Diving Coach. Although acting through the administration of the B.S-A.C., the services of the National Diving Coach are available to any club or organization in the United Kingdom, providing invaluable help and advice for inexperienced bodies that are just starting.

Thus man can now visit Neptune's domain, either as a spectator, viewing the scenery and taking snapshots, or as a scientist, extending the boundaries of the world. The future of the underwater world is, without a doubt, as exciting as the wildest science-fiction literature.

II. Getting Started

Advantages of Joining a Club

First of all, there is absolutely no advantage in diving alone. The author himself, has, on several occasions, received assistance from a fellow diver or snorkel cover, the lack of which could have had disastrous consequences.

Every year, in Britain alone, there are probably several hundred unreported cases of seemingly casual help: the diver who surfaces and hands his snorkel cover some excess weight, for example, or asks for a tow because he feels a little tired. These are common occurrences, any of which could prove hazardous if the diver were 'solo'; and this is apart from the many authentic rescues of divers in distress. It follows that, should you need assistance, the better trained and experienced the help available, the less chance there is of disaster. This book can only enable you to teach yourself *about* underwater swimming: attempting to teach yourself the practical side is to court the darker aspects of fate. Actual underwater experience should only be carried out under the supervision of a qualified instructor.

The most important attribute of a good diving club is the provision of training facilities and adequate instruction. Experienced members can provide advice and a fund of available knowledge. Occasionally, equipment can be hired or borrowed, enabling the embryo diver to experiment a little before purchasing his own. Courses of lectures on diving are given, and attendance is a necessity,

as the lectures form part of the training. The social side of
a club is usually in the form of 'dry' (as distinct from
swimming) meetings. Here, apart from the usual drone
of diving conversation, a film show or a lecture by a
prominent diving authority is often held. Apart from all
this, a club will have a diving programme planned. This
consists of various dives—some suitable for beginners,
others for more advanced members—arranged well in
advance, enabling you to fit in the type of dive most
suitable for your stage of training.

Throughout the world, clubs form a pool of diving
information in local areas. Clubs have been instrumental
in instituting safe diving procedure and campaigning
against laws that are unfair to underwater swimmers.
Many clubs contain groups that are active in the fields of
underwater photography, archaeology, biology, and other
aspects of the underwater world. They also provide, in
many cases, a service to the community by assisting the
police and local authorities with searches and information.

Diving on your own or with inexperienced partners can
be—indeed it is—dangerous. Diving with a club, you can
have much more fun, and in relative safety. Need more be
said?

Importance of Steam Swimming

Steam swimming—that is, natural swimming, without
artificial aids such as fins—is an important preliminary to
diving training. A competent swimmer will usually evolve
into a confident diver, for good watermanship is the first
essential in preventing that most dangerous swimming
hazard—panic. It is difficult to set a standard of swimming from which to progress to aqualung training, but
the British Sub-Aqua Club, for one, considers the matter
important enough to institute a swimming test. The

passing of this test is necessary before you are allowed to graduate to underwater swimming.

To start with, a good swimmer should be capable of a reasonable range of strokes: crawl, breast stroke, and a back stroke. Utilizing any of these strokes, he should be able to swim 300 yards in nine minutes or less. If, after completing the 300 yards, an additional 100 yards are completed while wearing a ten pound weight belt (provided, of course, that the swimmer has checked that he is of normal buoyancy), then a reasonable standard of swimming has been reached.

The ability to float, motionless, is a sign of good watermanship. It is not necessary to learn the difficult horizontal float; a vertical float held for several minutes indicates confidence and ability.

An item often introduced into swimming tests is treading water with the hands held above the head. Normally, a swimmer finds treading water quite easy, but when the hands are raised out of the water, the effect is to push the head under. A quicker, lighter leg-action is required to keep the head clear. The ability to perform this item for at least sixty seconds is also a sign of good watermanship.

A good jack-knife (Fig. 1) surface dive to the bottom of the pool to recover an object weighing five pounds will, when perfected, ensure that no trouble is experienced when the swimmer graduates to this same dive in the snorkeling tests.

It is perfectly natural for the novice diver to want to rush on to aqualung training as soon as possible; bothering to brush up on your swimming technique can prove tiresome when all that gleaming equipment lies by the side of the pool. But remember, when you are diving, you hold two lives in your hands—your own and your partner's—and you each have the right to expect a certain standard of competence in the other.

Importance of a Medical Examination

Although underwater swimming is a healthy sport, it is a hazardous activity for those whose physical or medical fitness is in doubt. Taking the various stresses into account (the loss of heat and energy owing to the lower temperature of the water, the high oxygen consumption, and the effects of pressure—even now not fully understood), it is easy to see why it is advisable that a medical examination should be a preliminary to starting underwater swimming.

Your doctor may—quite understandably, as this is a relatively new sport—be a little hazy as to what exactly is required, and here you must be of some assistance to him. Some afflictions spell obvious danger: heart disease, pulmonary tuberculosis, fits, asthma, and any weakening disease. Less obvious, at least from a non-diver's point of view, are ears, sinuses, and any tendency to headaches. Some people suffer occasional attacks of giddiness or fainting without ever bothering to consult their doctor; but even if the giddiness is mild and infrequent, the cause should be checked.

A medical examination is for your own good. Exhaustion, fainting, and vomiting are all distressing enough on land; underwater they can be fatal.

Mask

The mask is really the hub of underwater swimming. The haunting beauty of the underwater world and the mechanical efficiency of the demand valve would go unappreciated and unused if man were blind underwater —and he is. It is the mask that gives us the magic of sight underwater; all additional sub-aqua equipment merely serves to extend the range and application of the mask.

The reasons for the mask unblurring man's underwater vision are given in the section on physics, and need not be repeated. However, we do need to know something about the construction and design of masks to assist us in selecting an appropriate model.

First of all, goggles should never be worn for underwater swimming. A good mask should cover the eyes and nose, for when a swimmer descends, the water pressure causes the air inside the mask to compress, creating a dangerous squeeze on the eyes. This condition can easily be corrected by breathing into the mask through the nose; but this is impossible with goggles, which cover only the eyes. Also, water in the mask can be cleared by a vigorous snort through the nose—again impossible with goggles.

Having eliminated goggles, let us also dispose of another type of mask—the full-face mask that covers eyes, nose, and mouth. This type is manufactured with built-in snorkel tubes, giving its owner a fearsome appearance. The practical arguments against this assembly are as follows: a full-face mask renders it impossible to use underwater breathing apparatus, and, even if you do not want this facility, a further disadvantage is that this type is difficult to get off if it should flood; the built-in snorkels are equipped with various valves to prevent the water from entering the mask when its owner submerges, but snorkel valves have been vetoed by swimmers all over the world as being of little—if any—practical use.

When selecting your mask, choose a model that covers your eyes and nose. Place the mask on your face, with the straps hanging free, and inhale through your nose; if the fit is correct, the mask will stay on your face by the suction created. Probably many masks will pass this test for you, so buy the one which feels most comfortable.

The transparent front 'window' can be manufactured from plastic, which is tougher and safer than glass, but has the attendant disadvantages of being easy to scratch and difficult to prevent from misting up. More usually, the window will consist of toughened glass: a sandblasted mark to this effect should be present somewhere on its surface. The very popularity of toughened glass is proof of its suitability for underwater swimming. Some windows are equipped with laminated glass; this is an excellent material, but you should ensure that the laminite is not coming apart from the glass itself. This can be checked by examining the edge surface, which necessitates removing the window from the mask—a procedure likely to prove unwelcome in some shops.

Ordinary glass has actually been used for windows in some of the cheaper masks. The ease with which this can break or shatter, and the dangers involved, need not be elaborated on—sufficient to say that it would be better to stay out of the water than swim with such a face-piece.

Mask windows are usually clear, but some are tinted yellow. The idea is that yellow will increase the contrast of your vision underwater to enable you to see a little farther and clearer. No doubt this theory can be proved correct on the test bench, but it is difficult to judge any difference with the naked eye: the tinting does alter the underwater colour rendering, particularly in shallow water, and some people prefer this, but tinted windows still come a poor second in the popularity poll.

An innovation in the standard mask that has proved its worth is a device that enables you to pinch or close your nostrils. This can consist of a depression in the mask on each side of the nose, or externally operated levers that will clamp each nostril. Some people cannot clear their ears without sealing their nostrils (this sounds odd, but will be explained later), so the purchase of a mask with this 'improvement' depends upon the ease with which you can clear your ears. It is probably wisest to purchase a mask with this facility, because your physical condition can vary from day to day, and even the swimmer with 'clear' ears can, for no obvious reason, experience difficulty on odd days.

Another innovation, a built-in purge valve for clearing the mask of any accumulated water, is a luxury device. It works out cheaper to roll on your back or side and clear the orthodox way; furthermore, valves are devices that are best kept to a minimum, because they always seem to pack up when you need them most.

The holding strap of a mask should be of 'split-band' design. This, in effect, branches out into two bands at the rear of the head, resulting in a safer, more comfortable, and more secure fitting.

Fins

Without fins, the underwater swimmer would be an ungainly individual—probably descending with the aid of lead ballast and ascending with a form of buoyancy bag. Fins allow him to move through the water with a flexible ease, leaving his hands free to perform other tasks: the hands are rarely, if ever, used to assist propulsion.

In selecting your fins, comfort is the first consideration. A loose flipper will chafe and cause blisters, while a fit that is too snug will restrict circulation and cause cramp. When purchasing, bear in mind whether the fins will be used on bare feet or over the bootees of a wet (or dry) suit.

Broadly, there are two varieties of fins—those with a full foot fitting, and the type with an open heel held on by straps. The most popular are the full fitting: these transform the fin into an integral part of your leg and, if they fit correctly, are safer. The open heel and strap fitting has its advocates, but the point where the fin starts—or is it ceases?—can chafe the foot; also, if a strap should break, the swimmer would be helpless unless proficient in the technique of single-fin swimming.

Black fins are usually made from a heavy, rigid rubber. Coloured types are more pliable, and often float—an obvious advantage.

The blade area of the fin is important. While a large blade gives powerful propulsion on the feet of a swimmer with strong legs, it can prove exhausting to a lesser mortal. The same is also true of the rigidity of the fins: the rigid type are faster but require a good deal of effort, and the flexible variety are slower but easier on the legs.

Snorkel

The basic equipment of an underwater swimmer could be considered as just mask and fins, but the snorkel tube has proved such a practical success that it is now an integral part of the equipment. In fact, its use has coined a title in underwater swimming, 'snorkel diver', indicating a swimmer who is using only fins, mask, and snorkel.

In use, a snorkel allows the user to breathe easily while swimming on the surface face down, which eliminates the tiresome necessity of continually raising the head to breathe. It is also invaluable to aqualung divers when a choppy sea sends water washing over the mouth, and the diver either has no air left in his cylinder, or wishes to conserve the air he has.

Basically, a snorkel is a straight tube with a 'U' bend at one end to which is fitted a mouthpiece. Sometimes, it is equipped with valves that prevent water entering, but these are of no real use. The snorkel with a plain, open end requires little practice to use properly, and is an uncomplicated design with which nothing can go wrong. In theory, a snorkel tube with a large bore is difficult, even impossible, to clear water from, and a tube that is too long is medically undesirable owing to the excessive amount of exhaled air that would be re-inhaled. In fact, no snorkel sold in a shop would comply with these specifications; the selection of a snorkel tube is dictated by the comfort of fit.

Nose Clips and Ear Plugs

Underwater swimmers should not need their noses held closed; apart from the disturbance of vision, they should be just as comfortable with their masks off as on. If a diver relies on a nose clip, and an accident dislodges both mask and nose clip, the consequences could be fatal. It takes very little practice—finning along the surface without a mask and breathing through a snorkel—to get used to breathing through a mouthpiece while the nostrils are in contact with water.

Ear plugs are doubly dangerous. As the underwater swimmer submerges, the pressure of water will drive the plugs into the ears.

Although possibly of some use to the surface steam swimmer, the underwater swimmer should avoid both of these articles.

Snorkel Diving: the Basic Technique

Let us imagine that you are by the side of a swimming-pool, awaiting your initiation into snorkel diving.

Sit on the edge of the pool and put your fins on. Next take hold of your mask, spit on the inside of the glass window and rub the spittle all over the glass, then rinse the mask in the water: this treatment will prevent the window from misting up when you are under water. If your snorkel is attached to the outside of your mask strap (a special attachment is manufactured for this), then it only remains to fit the mouthpiece in; if, on the other hand, your snorkel does not have this attachment, then

slide the snorkel under the mask strap before popping the
other end into your mouth.

Now slide into the water, and hang on to the side or a
ladder. While doing this, keep your face in the water,
observing the underwater scene around you and getting
used to breathing through the snorkel. When you feel
quite comfortable, release your hold and swim a couple
of lengths. Your legs will tend to make a bicycling action,
but try to avoid this: attempt to keep your knees reasonably rigid, your hands held next to your sides, and try not
to let your heels thrash in the air.

The next step is to learn to clear your snorkel. Stand
in the shallow end at the point where the water reaches
your chest. Now either lean forward or bend your knees
until your snorkel is completely under water; straighten
up and clear the water with a sharp blow. The first few
attempts will probably make you cough and splutter—
but persevere. The inhalation immediately after clearing
the tube should be a smooth, gentle one: if you 'snatch'
(that is, inhale sharply), you may inhale a few drops of
water that remain in the tube, making you cough and
ruining the effort.

As has been mentioned, a mask that comes off—
perhaps by an accidental knock or a strap snapping—is a
great danger to the untrained diver. If mastered, the
following exercise will ensure, in the event of such a
mishap occuring, that you remain calm and competent.

Retire to one end of the pool; remove your mask and
leave it on the side. Now swim a length, face down,
breathing through the snorkel (you will have to hold the
snorkel in place, or else it will dip into the water). Do not
pinch your nostrils shut with your free hand, and keep
your eyes open: it is a good plan to follow one of the
black lines that usually run the length of a pool, as your
blurred vision will see little else. This exercise is invaluable to your future training and diving. If you find it

difficult at first, don't try for too long: the chemicals in the water will make your eyes bloodshot. Even after you have mastered this procedure, it is wise to give it a run through once in a while—say, every third month.

You should now have reached a stage where you are ready to attempt mask clearing. If your mask comes off, at depth, and you recover it, it is obviously necessary to clear the mask of water; most likely, it will only be a slight leak, with a little water irritating your nostrils. The method of clearing is the same in both cases.

Go to the ladder at the deep end, leaving your fins and snorkel by the side. Take a deep breath, and descend the ladder until the top of your head is about six inches below water. While holding on securely with one hand and both feet (to prevent yourself floating back to the surface), use your free hand to pull your mask sufficiently away for it to flood; then ease your mask back into position. Now tilt your head back so that you are looking up towards the surface; place your free hand along the top of the mask and press gently; then snort through your nose.

The principle is that, as you breathe into the mask, the air, being lighter than water, rises and accumulates at the top of the mask: it cannot escape because your hand is holding the mask firm against your forehead. As more air is released into the mask, it occupies more and more space, driving the water steadily downward until, when air starts to emit from the bottom of the mask, the water has been completely cleared.

Once you have the hang of it, you will find that you do not require an explosion of bubbles to clear your mask, as this only wastes air—an important consideration when diving at depth. The well-trained underwater swimmer should be able to clear a fully flooded mask at least three times on a single lungful of air. If at first the procedure seems a lot to complete on a single breath,

then fill the mask and put it on before you descend the
ladder.

Whether aqualung or snorkel diving—or spear-fishing
—you should endeavour to adjust your weight belt so
that you are slightly buoyant on the surface. This, however, poses a minor problem when you attempt to submerge: a little downward thrust is needed, which is
provided by your legs in the following manner. Snorkel
along the surface; (Fig. 1.1) taking a light breath, plunge
the top half of your body downwards, as if you were
trying to touch your toes; at the same time, throw both
legs up into the air (Fig. 1.2). The weight of your legs
will push you neatly under water with scarcely a splash, if
you have performed the action (Fig. 1.3)—a jack-knife
dive— correctly.

While practising the jack-knife dive, you may note, at a
certain depth, a pressure or ache in your ear-drum. The
cause is explained in the chapter on physics; we are more
concerned here with how to eliminate this discomfort.

The various methods of alleviating pressure on the
ear-drums are all known as 'clearing the ears', and they
should be applied as soon as there is any sign of pressure
—don't wait until the onset of pain. There are three
methods to try initially, these being suitable for people
whose ears are relatively easy to clear, which consist of
swallowing, pretending to yawn, and snorting into the
mask. If you are one of the fortunates who can clear their
ears by the above methods, then experiment and find the
one that suits you best. Should none of these actions have
any effect (and this is generally the case), attempt the
following procedure. Seal the nostrils (this is where the
mask designed for this facility comes in) and try to blow
out gently through the nose. If this does not work, try
waggling your jaws as you try to blow. Don't blow hard
if you find things difficult, for this can damage your ear-
drum.

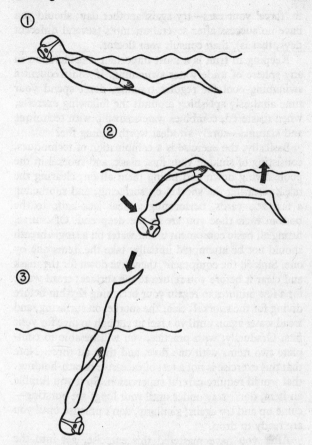

Fig. 1. Sequence of a clean surface dive.

If none of these methods succeed in clearing your ears, there could be several possible explanations. You might, for instance, be suffering from a cold; or catarrh might be blocking certain vital passages. In any case, don't try to 'force' your ears—try again another day; should you have no success after several attempts (several different days, that is), then consult your doctor.

Keeping in trim is a most important consideration in any sphere of underwater swimming. If you frequent a swimming-pool for regular training, don't spend your time aimlessly splashing around: the following exercise, when mastered, combines watermanship with technique and stamina—surely an ideal worth aiming for?

Basically, the exercise is a combination of techniques, consisting of sinking your fins, mask, and snorkel in the pool; diving down and fitting them all on; clearing the mask; clearing the snorkel on surfacing; and snorkeling a fast 200 yards, performing a clear jack-knife to the bottom each time you are in the deep end. Of course, fitting all basic equipment under water on a single breath should not be attempted initially: take the items one by one. Sink all the equipment, then dive down for the mask and clear it before you return to the surface; tread water for a few minutes to regain your breathing rhythm before diving for the snorkel; clear the snorkel on surfacing, and tread water again until you feel fit enough to dive for your fins. Gradually, with practice, you will be able to complete two items with one dive, and then all three. Note that this exercise is not a test of excessive breath-holding: that would require careful supervision. So if you fumble an item, don't stay under until your lungs are bursting— come up and try again; similarly, don't practise until you are ready to drop.

After you have mastered this exercise, get into the habit of fitting your basic equipment under water; and complete a good surface swim every time you visit the pool, as a preliminary to anything else you might have lined up.

III. Physics and Medical

PART ONE—PHYSICS OF DIVING

The mere mention of physics is usually enough to conjure up a feeling of apprehension; but the free-diver needs a certain amount of knowledge regarding the laws relating to, and composition of, water in order to understand the problems of buoyancy adjustment, decompression, embolism, ear-clearing, and the various ailments that can beset him while in his liquid environment. It is important, therefore, not to gloss over this chapter. The information that pressure is doubled at a depth of 33 feet may not sound as exciting as the location of a wreck, but it is of greater importance to the diver who wishes to reach a ripe old age.

Atmospheric air consists of a variety of gases: approximately 78 per cent nitrogen, 21 per cent oxygen, 1 per cent argon, less than 0·4 per cent carbon dioxide, and smaller quantities of other gases. Virtually held in place by the gravitational pull of the earth, the mantle of air that surrounds us exerts a pressure relative to the distance from the earth's centre—the farther away, the less the pressure. At sea level, the pressure of air measures 14·7 pounds per square inch (p.s.i.), and is termed, as a standard unit, one atmosphere. This pressure is exerted equally from all directions, and the human body has become adjusted to it—indeed, it is not normally noticed until a malfunction like a heavy cold or sinus trouble is thrust upon us.

Air is compressible: thus, by virtue of its own pressure or 'weight' the air gets progressively denser as it nears sea level. For example, although exerting 14·7 p.s.i. at sea level, the atmospheric pressure at the top of Mount Everest is less than 4 p.s.i. It is this compressibility that enables the free-diver to invade the deep. A vast quantity of air can be forced into a cylinder, giving the diver a portable supply of air that the advertising boys would probably call 'condensed cream of air'.

Water is 800 times denser than air—one cubic foot of sea water weighs approximately 64 pounds (fresh water a little less)—and is incompressible. This means that the water at the bottom of the ocean is no denser than that near the surface, and that the enormous pressures existing at the bottom are the result of the sheer weight of the water above. The difference in density is shown by the fact that a layer of air many miles thick produces a pressure of 14·7 p.s.i., while this same pressure is obtained, in water, at a depth of only 33 feet.

Pressure under water is expressed by using one atmosphere as a standard unit. There are two methods of using underwater pressure calculations: 'gauge' pressure, which ignores the pressure of atmospheric air and indicates the pressure of water only, and 'absolute', which includes the unit of one atmosphere existing at sea level. A diver at a depth of 33 feet would thus be subject to a pressure of one atmosphere, 14·7 p.s.i. gauge, or else two atmospheres, 29·4 p.s.i. absolute. In diving, an otherwise unqualified calculation is usually assumed to read absolute.

The human body, being composed of practically incompressible fluids and solids, is relatively unaffected by pressure provided it has access to all body surfaces. And there's the rub. The body has a number of internal cavities (lungs, sinus spaces, inner ear spaces) and if pressure is applied to the body externally—as when swimming under water on a single breath with no apparatus—these cavities are subjected to a compressive effect which can, in certain circumstances, cause pain and damage. What is required, is the introduction into these cavities of a pressure that will compensate the external force of water; this is where the cylinder of compressed air comes in.

At a depth of 66 feet, a free-diver has a pressure of three atmospheres absolute (44·1 p.s.i.) applied to his external surfaces. As he sucks on his mouthpiece, his demand valve will regulate the flow of air from his cylinder to this same pressure. Provided there is no body malfunction, such as a heavy cold, this compressed air will flood the internal cavities, compensating the external pressure, and no discomfort will be felt. Such is the miracle of the demand valve.

Breathing compressed air is not without its complications (these are dealt with in the medical section) but they all evolve from the following laws. At a depth of 33 feet, a diver receives air that is compressed to a pressure of two atmospheres absolute—double the pressure he breathes at sea level—to compensate for the external water pressure. At this moment, his lungs will contain twice as much air—in compressed form—as he would require on the surface; they will obviously contain twice as much nitrogen, oxygen, carbon dioxide, etc. Farther down, at 66 feet, he will be breathing air compressed to three atmospheres, with a proportional increase in the gases just mentioned. The deeper he goes, the higher the compression of the air he breathes, and the greater his intake of the gases that the air consists of. It is this bodily saturation of various gases, and the expansion of this compressed air that takes place when the diver rises to the surface, that can give rise to narcosis, embolism, and other sub-aquatic ailments.

B

Vision Under Water

The first thing that the novice diver usually notices under water is that objects appear closer and larger than they really are. This illusion will make a subject 10 feet away appear to be at a distance of approximately 7 feet. The reason for this is that the eye is adjusted to operate in air; if placed under water, the focusing range becomes too short to utilize, and the whole scene is recorded as a dull blur. When a mask is worn, the eye is once again focusing in air, and vision becomes clear, but as the light travels through three mediums (water, glass, and air) on its way to the eye, the illusion of 'nearness' occurs. In practice, however, this is only disconcerting on the first few dives, for the brain soon adjusts to this visual distortion.

Sound

If the diver removes his mouthpiece under water and attempts to talk, the result is an unintelligible gabble. Although sound travels at over 1,000 feet per second in air, and five times faster in water, their physical differences are such as to prevent transmission of the greater part of sound through air into water—and vice versa. As the diver's words originate in the medium of air (the throat), they are nullified at the air-water contact when they leave the mouth.

However, the underwater world is not completely silent: the diver can utilize sound by striking two hard surfaces. Two rocks in contact will produce a clicking sound that can be heard for a short distance, as can the ringing sound produced by striking a cylinder with a metal object such as a knife. Sound produced in this manner can be fashioned into a simple set of signals.

PART TWO—PHYSICAL AND MEDICAL

Exhaustion

Of the many dangerous conditions and ailments that can befall the free-diver, exhaustion is undoubtedly the most common. Luckily, only a small percentage ever suffer the bends, narcosis, or other exotic-sounding disorders, but every underwater swimmer experiences, at some time during his diving life, the hazard of fatigue.

There are several causes of exhaustion, including panic, cold, and over-exertion, but they can all be reduced by careful planning and regular training. A prime cause is, without doubt, overweight. A long snorkel home can be tiring, and it is here, on the surface and out of air, that the diver is most vulnerable. If the diver is too heavy at the surface, his snorkel will, on the long plod back, drop lower and lower into the water until a mouthful is inhaled and he panics. On the surface, a diver should be weighted so that he is a pound or two—no more—buoyant and just floats comfortably.

Although fins give the underwater swimmer greater power, even these articles of propulsion will create little impression against a fast current. If things go awry and you have to battle your way out of a swift flow, don't attempt to swim directly against the current, but across it in a diagonal direction.

The demand valve, like most things, is not perfect: there is a fractional time lag on inhalation that is not noticed in normal use; but when over exertion causes heavy breathing, a stage can be reached when insufficient air is being supplied. In this condition, the diver should cease all movement and relax; if possible, a position should be attained whereby the demand valve is below the level of the chest, as this will increase the flow of air slightly. The important thing is to try to restore a normal breathing rhythm.

Cold and fatigue go hand in hand, and are dealt with in the section on diving under ice. It is impossible to tell whether a person would, or would not, panic under certain conditions, but it is possible to cut down the chances. A well-trained diver is more likely to go through procedure automatically in an emergency—so don't fall out of practice with the drills: utilize your swimming-pool for constant revision and training. It only needs one emergency to have made it all worth while.

Ears and Sinus

A diver usually has one particular physical indication that he is being subjected to above-average pressure: the sensation in his ears, or, more correctly, the middle ear space. To understand this condition correctly, a basic knowledge of the construction of the ear and hearing mechanism is needed.

The ear is basically divided into three parts: the outer ear, which is the visible fleshy appendage and includes the canal that leads to the ear-drum; the middle ear, which lies beyond the ear drum and consists of an air space with a tube—The Eustachian tube—leading to the throat; and another ear-drum, which connects to the internal ear. Briefly, sound travels along the outer ear canal and vibrations echo across the middle ear space to the internal ear-drum, and thence to the internal ear, where hearing takes place.

The Eustachian tube is the only contact that the middle ear space has with atmospheric air, and its function is to keep the air pressure adjusted in this chamber. If the Eustachian tube in normal use becomes blocked or closed—through catarrh or swollen membranes—the middle ear space becomes sealed, air is slowly absorbed, and the pressure drops below atmospheric; the outer ear-drum is then subjected to external atmospheric pressure, resulting—common to many people when suffering with a cold—in ear-ache.

In diving, this problem is magnified and speeded up; pressure changes so abruptly that the Eustachian tube is forced shut, isolating the middle ear. On descending, the quickly increasing external pressure causes pain and, if the descent continues with a closed Eustachian tube, the ear-drum will puncture or tear. Fortunately, the average person can perform a simple ear clearing action: a few can do this by trying to yawn; usually, however, the nostrils are held closed and a gentle blow attempted through the nose. Both, or either, of these actions should open the Eustachian tube and should be carried out when slight pressure is felt—don't wait until the onset of pain.

Should an ear-drum perforate, there are various symptoms. The most dangerous occurs when water trickles through the perforation; apart from the possibility of infection, cold water in the middle ear can cause sickness, dizziness, and a complete loss of the sense of balance. In this case, the diver will not even know the direction of the surface and should, if possible, grab hold of something solid. When the water in the middle ear has warmed up to body temperature, the sense of balance will return. However, while in this condition, if you feel the hands of your partner holding you, you may be sure that he is bringing you to the surface—so don't struggle or hold your breath (see Air Embolism).

Other symptoms of a perforated ear-drum are: feeling bubbles escape from the ear—in which case get out of the water; and a discharge of blood from the ear, with perhaps little or no pain.

In all cases, the ear should be covered—not plugged—with an antiseptic cloth or lint and a doctor seen immediately. Provided there are no complications, a small

puncture will often heal within several days, but keep out
of the water until the doctor gives the O.K.

The human skull has several natural air spaces (sinuses)
located within its frontal section. Their function is
dubious and outside the scope of this book, but they can
create a problem identical to that of the middle ear. The
sinuses have connections (called ostia) through to the
nose which perform the same function as the Eustachian
tube. When blocked, they cannot equalise pressure;
severe pain will be felt on descending, and a little blood
may be discharged into the face mask. Sinuses cannot be
cleared while on a dive; if pain is felt, diving should be
abandoned for the day. A cold is probably the cause—in
which case, diving should never have commenced. In the
event of a sinus condition persisting for several days, a
doctor should be consulted.

Drinking

There are two types of liquid refreshment that can affect
a diver's performance or condition adversely. The most
obvious is alcohol. The effects of intoxicants while the
body is subjected to pressure have not been fully investi-
gated, and it could prove dangerous to experiment along
these lines! Little need be said about the befuddling
mental action experienced when drinking intoxicants—
and the probable danger to the diver. So, if you're drinking, don't dive.

Of more subtle danger is the carbonated fizzy drink. A
sparkling drink will not 'fizz' while in a sealed bottle,
being restrained by the pressure built up in the small air
space. Should a diver consume a carbonated drink before
submerging, the pressure, while underwater, will tend to
subdue the drink, and none of those disconcerting burps
will occur: that is, until the diver surfaces. Then the
'fizz' will be released. By this time, the liquid may have

travelled far in its journey to the bladder, and pockets of carbonated gases will form, sometimes causing severe discomfort. Sparkling drinks of any type should not be consumed for at least two hours prior to a dive.

Cramp

Cramp is a painful spasm of a muscle, or group of muscles, usually affecting the lower limbs. It is of greater danger to the steam swimmer than the diver, unless the latter is on the surface, out of air, and overweighted—a situation he should not get into. The spasm may last a few seconds or several minutes and can be brought on by exertion, cold, or working in a confined or awkward position. A meal eaten before a dive can divert blood to the abdominal organs, leaving the muscles relatively short of blood and liable to cramp.

If cramp occurs, stretch the limb and rub the affected part. This is a signal that it is time to leave the water. Out of the water, massage the area and, if the cramp persists, apply heat.

Air Embolism

From our section on physics, we know that a diver at a depth of 33 feet has double the normal quantity of air compressed into his lungs to compensate for the increased water pressure. When a diver ascends, the water pressure decreases, and the air in his lungs starts to expand. Should the diver ascend rapidly, or while holding his breath, the pressure in the lung becomes greater than the external water pressure, over-expanding the lung; air may be forced into the lung walls, forming bubbles that can enter the circulation, blocking and rupturing small blood vessels.

Prevention is better than cure, so always ascend at a

steady pace: the inhalation should be short and the exhalation long. Should it become necessary to surface rapidly (an air failure for instance) the mouth should be kept open and a continuous exhalation carried out—the faster the ascent, the swifter the exhalation. Panic can cause the throat to seize up, preventing the air from escaping freely; but if this occurs, it is usually the result of poor or inadequate training.

The symptoms of an embolism are many: hoarse throat or chest, muzzy speech, tight chest, dizziness, blood or froth from the mouth, numbness or paralysis of the extremities, unconsciousness, convulsions. There is no treatment that can be applied on the spot. Keep the subject warm, and rush him to the nearest recompression chamber. Speed is of vital importance; a few minutes can make the difference between life and death.

Another ailment that can arise, spontaneous pneumothorax, is the result of air being trapped in the cavity between chest and lung. On ascent, the expanding air can collapse the lung and even displace the heart. Symptoms include pains in the chest, extreme shortness of breath, irregular pulse, and dark discoloration of the skin. As the treatment includes puncturing the chest with a needle to release the trapped air, immediate medical attention is necessary.

The Bends

Of all the diving afflictions, this could be called the most glamorous; it is certainly well publicised in the popular Press. The bends derives its name from the contorted positions that its crippling pain forces a sufferer to adopt. More divers—particularly professionals—have been maimed or killed by the bends than by any other medical diving hazard.

The basic cause is a condition termed nitrogen

absorbtion. A diver breathing compressed air will be absorbing an above average concentration of each gas that the air is composed of. In the case of nitrogen, the excess will normally dissolve into the blood as the diver ascends and will be breathed out through the lungs. However, should a diver exceed a certain depth for a prolonged period of time, the body absorbs nitrogen to a level at which the following condition can occur.

As the diver rises to the surface, the excess nitrogen may come out of solution faster than the blood can carry it away, forming small bubbles in the tissues and the blood. These bubbles can lodge in almost any part of the body, causing the severe pain that gives rise to the bends. The only treatment is to recompress the bubbles back into solution, and decompress slowly. This procedure is carried out in a recompression chamber, of which there are precious few; for this reason, the address and telephone number of the nearest recompression chamber should be in the possession of every diving excursion.

Symptoms usually consist of pain in the joints of the limbs, itching or swelling of the skin, dizziness, shortness of breath, and, in the case of spinal bends, paralysis. If the bubbles are large enough, they can cause a blockage of the heart, with obvious results.

There are two methods of avoiding the bends. The simplest—and safest—procedure is avoiding the maximum nitrogen absorbtion level. If a depth deeper than 30 feet is to be attempted, then no more than 40 cubic feet of air—the equivalent of one standard 7-inch cylinder—should be consumed in any 12-hour period. Alternatively, if a maximum depth limit of 33 feet is imposed, it is impossible to reach a dangerous level of absorbtion, and an unlimited time can be spent under water.

Should deeper, longer dives be contemplated, then a

dangerous level of nitrogen absorbtion might be reached, and this excess nitrogen would have to be gradually dissipated by a procedure known as decompressing. This entails ascending at a speed no faster than 60 feet per minute, and stopping at certain depths for regulated periods of time laid down by decompression tables. For instance, if a dive to a depth of 150 feet is planned, we will find, by reference to the decompression tables, that if we exceed a certain time at this depth, including the descent, then our ascent of 60 feet per minute will have to be interrupted when 10 feet from the surface by a stop of several minutes. This additional time has to be taken into consideration when estimating the supply of air needed.

As a rule, only one dive a day requiring decompression should be carried out. Should a second dive become necessary, then decompress for the combined times and deepest dive (e.g. first dive, 40 minutes at 150 feet; second dive, 25 minutes at 75 feet: for the second dive, refer to the decompression tables, using a time of 65 minutes and a depth of 150 feet).

Nitrogen Narcosis

This is another dangerous side-effect of nitrogen breathed under pressure. Although given colourful names (such as 'rapture of the deep' and 'diver's alcohol') nitrogen narcosis is a possible danger to all divers working at a depth greater than 100 feet. The effect, as with the bends, varies with different people. Indeed, it varies from day to day in the same person, and the symptoms can commence at any depth from 100 feet down.

The symptoms are similar to alcoholic intoxication: every little co-ordinated action becomes muddled, thinking becomes confused, and the instinct for self-preservation can disappear. This has resulted in divers happily

swimming down to depths greater than they would
normally consider—perhaps under the delusion that
they were surfacing—or removing the mouthpiece, considering it no longer necessary. Little imagination is
required to realise the danger open to the diver while
in this condition. The symptoms will vanish if an ascent,
often of only a few feet, is made, and no after-effects
occur.

Should you experience loss of judgement or control
while under water, make an immediate but steady ascent
until the condition clears, and do not return to that depth
the same day. If your partner shows symptoms and, in
addition, is reluctant to ascend, don't attempt to force
the action—at least, not from the front. Swim around to
his rear, grasp his cylinder, and fin upwards.

Anoxia, Hyperventilation, and Reduced Breathing

One of the first symptoms of oxygen lack (anoxia) is
unconsciousness; the danger, should this happen under
water and with no help near by, is obvious.

Probably the most common cause of blackout under
water among spear-fishermen is hyperventilation. This
comes from several minutes' really deep breathing, and
affects the body by reducing the proportion of carbon
dioxide. After hyperventilation, a snorkel diver can last
longer underwater; the normal warning—the desire to
breathe—that is triggered off by a carbon dioxide build-
up is delayed by the hyperventilating and flushing of this
gas. Thus, a well-trained spear-fisherman can reach a
pitch where there is a very thin dividing line between
the desire to breathe and a blackout.

Anoxia can also strike the diver who tries to economise
on air. Although a shallow, reduced breathing-rate that

verges on semi-breath-holding will reduce the consumption of air from the cylinder, this is an unwise way
of trying to extend a dive. Reduced breathing also reduces
the supply of oxygen; in certain conditions, it could
easily lead to a blackout.

A lack of oxygen can also be brought about by a faulty
or contaminated air supply.

Oxygen Poisoning

The compressed-air cylinders of the modern free-diver
are often referred to in the popular Press as containing
oxygen—a dangerous misnomer. This is no doubt a
throw-back to the Second World War, when frogmen
used cylinders containing pure oxygen; this was continually re-breathed, the exhaled carbon dioxide being
removed via an absorbent, so that no tell-tale bubbles
were given off to inform the enemy. Although of use to
military authorities, pure oxygen should never be used in
cylinders: indeed, the B.S-A.C. and many other clubs
have banned the use of oxygen re-breathing apparatus,
and for the following reasons:

Pure oxygen, when breathed for too long a period, has
marked harmful effects. Breathed under a pressure of two
atmospheres or more—a depth of 33 feet, or deeper, for
the diver—the symptoms of oxygen poisoning can
develop immediately; as these symptoms include cough-
ing, vomiting, convulsion, and unconsciousness, the
reasons for the ban are obvious.

Oxygen poisoning can also occur in the free-diver using
compressed air: at a depth of nearly 300 feet, the amount
of oxygen in the air supply would sum two atmospheres.
As the amateur diver should not even contemplate depths
in this region, the problem should not arise.

Carbon Dioxide Poisoning

Normal atmospheric air contains less than 0·4 per cent carbon dioxide; after exhalation, this will increase to over 4 per cent. If the breath is held, this increased percentage of carbon dioxide will build up and, as this gas has a direct effect on respiration, stimulate the desire to breathe.

When the inhaled air contains more than 2 per cent carbon dioxide—at atmospheric pressure—breathlessness will occur. A further increase will cause heavy panting, headache, and exhaustion. At a 10 per cent concentration, unconsciousness and death are not very far away. This is one of the reasons why a free-diver will become breathless after comparatively little exertion under water, for, at 66 feet, three times the normal amount of carbon dioxide is being inhaled, and this renders the diver more prone to fatigue.

Carbon Monoxide Poisoning

Carbon monoxide will contaminate the air supply if the exhaust outlet of a petrol-driven air compressor is too close to the air intake; if other exhaust fumes are present, as in a garage; or if the particular oil used in the compressor has reached a flashing-point.

As with most other gases, the detrimental effects of carbon monoxide in the body will increase with pressure. A small percentage of this gas can cause sickness and headache, while, at the other end of the scale, a large percentage can bring on unconsciousness and death. Any time that a free-diver experiences drowsiness, giddiness, palpitations, or nausea, carbon monoxide poisoning should be suspected. The face of a victim will be flushed, and he will have a rapid or irregular pulse. The treatment is plenty of fresh air—and artificial respiration if breathing has stopped.

IV. Essential Equipment

The equipment described here is the very basic apparatus
needed to transform the skin-diver, who uses only fins,
mask, and snorkel, into a free-diver capable of staying
under water for comparatively long periods. Now the
whole world has a hazy, roughly accurate grasp of how
the modern free-diver breathes under water: he sucks on
a mouthpiece, drawing air through the corrugated tubes
from the cylinder of compressed air strapped on his
back. What is not so apparent is the mechanism that
intercepts the corrugated tubes before they arrive at the
cylinder; known as a demand valve (Fig. 2) or, in
America, as a regulator, it adjusts the flow of air as the
diver inhales to the correct quantity and pressure.

Principles and Selection of the Demand
  Valve

The operation of a demand valve is simplicity itself.
Basically, the nerve centre is a large rubber diaphragm,
one side of which is in contact with the water, and the
other with the air from the cylinder. The weight of water
creates a pressure on the external face, causing it to bulge
inwards; this bulge actuates a lever, releasing air from
the cylinder into the space contained by the internal face
of the diaphragm. As the air released reaches the same
pressure as the external water, the bulge is pressed back,
easing the pressure on the actuating lever. It is this
principle that allows the free-diver to draw air, for his

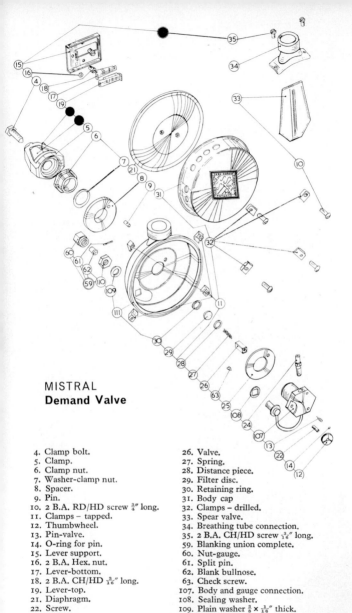

MISTRAL
Demand Valve

4. Clamp bolt.
5. Clamp.
6. Clamp nut.
7. Washer-clamp nut.
8. Spacer.
9. Pin.
10. 2 B.A. RD/HD screw $\frac{3}{4}''$ long.
11. Clamps – tapped.
12. Thumbwheel.
13. Pin-valve.
14. O-ring for pin.
15. Lever support.
16. 2 B.A. Hex. nut.
17. Lever-bottom.
18. 2 B.A. CH/HD $\frac{3}{16}''$ long.
19. Lever-top.
21. Diaphragm.
22. Screw.
24. Bullnose.
25. Joint washer.

26. Valve.
27. Spring.
28. Distance piece.
29. Filter disc.
30. Retaining ring.
31. Body cap.
32. Clamps – drilled.
33. Spear valve.
34. Breathing tube connection.
35. 2 B.A. CH/HD screw $\frac{5}{16}''$ long.
59. Blanking union complete.
60. Nut-gauge.
61. Split pin.
62. Blank bullnose.
63. Check screw.
107. Body and gauge connection.
108. Sealing washer.
109. Plain washer $\frac{3}{8} \times \frac{1}{16}''$ thick.
110. Nut.
111. Body case.

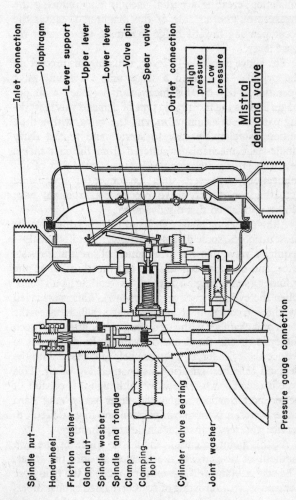

Inlet connection
Diaphragm
Lever support
Upper lever
Lower lever
Valve pin
Spear valve
Outlet connection

	High pressure	Low pressure

Mistral demand valve

Spindle nut
Handwheel
Friction washer
Gland nut
Spindle washer
Spindle and tongue
Clamp
Clamping bolt
Cylinder valve seating
Joint washer

Pressure gauge connection

Fig. 3. Cut-through diagram of the Siebe/Gorman 'Mistral' demand valve.

inhalation, creating a partial vacuum and reducing the pressure on the air side of the diaphragm, causes the accompanying inward bulge to actuate the cylinder release lever.

The above principle—a lever, actuating air direct from the cylinder—is termed a stage, and a demand valve operating solely by this mechanism is called a single-stage. This is the most basic type of demand valve: working parts are at a minimum, and the valve, with a little tuition, is relatively easy to service and repair. Early single-stage mechanisms suffered from the fact that a relatively strong suck was needed to start the flow of air; innovations, however, such as longer or articulated actuating levers and more precise construction, have almost eliminated this disadvantage.

Although a single-stage demand valve is admirable for most purposes, some divers—particularly professionals—require a valve that has a minimum of breathing resistance, and one that can use the last breath of air in the cylinder (some single-stage valves tend to 'pull hard' when the cylinder pressure drops low). This is achieved by the introduction of another stage, which takes the form of a chamber with a reducing valve, fitting between the cylinder and the demand chamber. Its purpose is to reduce the cylinder air pressure before it passes into the demand chamber, ensuring a smoother flow of air. This type is called a two-stage valve; although it is capable of better performances when the diver is working hard under water, it is more complicated and more difficult to service and repair than its single-stage brother.

At this point, mention should be made of the two methods of discharging the exhaled air into the water. The original (and still the most popular) is the twin hose demand valve. Consisting of two corrugated rubber tubes, one tube carries air from the demand valve to the mouthpiece, while the other conveys the exhaled air from the mouthpiece back to the demand valve, where it is released into the water. The second method is that of the single hose, or split-stage, demand valve, which is of two-stage construction. The first stage is fitted at the cylinder head; a small bore tube leads off from here to the mouthpiece, where the diaphragm and second stage are located; the exhaled air is released via two metal tubes just under the chin. Some divers do not like the heavy mouthpiece of the single hose valve, nor the fact that exhaled air is released around the face; but this type is cheaper to manufacture, and, as this makes them a more economical proposition, their popularity is increasing. Also, some divers prefer the neatness of the single hose.

There are, then, three types of demand valve generally available, and their relative merits are shown in the table on page 40.

It is obviously important that the free-diver should be able to tell when the air in his cylinder is low. There are two mechanisms available that perform this function: the pressure gauge, and the air reserve system. The former is attached to the demand valve via a high-pressure hose; a needle on the face indicates the pressure (or amount) of air available at any stage of the dive. In the air reserve system, the air becomes hard to draw when the air pressure is very low, and a reserve lever has to be pulled to obtain the remaining air, thus warning the diver that it is time to ascend. Although the air reserve method may seem to possess an advantage inasmuch as it physically informs the diver that he is low on air—he may be too absorbed to look at a gauge—in practice this does not work out; with little experience, a diver will automatically keep a constant check on his gauge. Furthermore, a gauge performs three functions: it will inform you when you are low on air; of the amount of air available throughout the dive; and of the amount of air available before you dive. If the last-named should seem

Type	Advantages	Disadvantages
Twin hose single-stage	Relatively cheap. Easy to maintain and repair.	Tends to pull hard when cylinder pressure is low or when diver is breathing heavily. The corrugated air hoses can be punctured.
Twin hose two-stage	Easy air flow, even when cylinder pressure is low and when breathing heavily.	The most expensive type of demand valve. Difficult to repair. The corrugated air hoses can be punctured.
Single hose two-stage	Cheapest type of demand valve. More compact than twin hose models. The air hose is almost impossible to puncture.	Mouthpiece is heavy. Exhaled air is released around the face.

unimportant, it should be remembered that errors may occur when compressor crews are busy at the height of the season: cylinders may be returned only half charged, or almost empty, by mistake, and bobbing in a boat several miles out at sea is not the time to find this out. A gauge gives an instant check that your cylinder is fully charged; an air reserve will only operate when the air is dangerously low.

Demand valves need regular maintenance. After each dive, thoroughly rinse valve and hoses in fresh water, holding a finger over the filter at the back to ensure that water does not enter at this point. Store away from excessive heat and from sharp objects that might cut or puncture a hose. A demand valve should not be fastened to a cylinder until just before the dive, and it should be removed immediately after; if left on a cylinder, it can easily be damaged. Working parts wear and rubber perishes, so ensure that your demand valve is overhauled every winter, even if apparently in perfect working order.

Cylinders

Cylinders provide the means of housing the compressed air in a portable form, enabling the free-diver to exist under water for indefinite periods. Usually manufactured from steel alloy, cylinders come in a variety of sizes and, for aqualung use in the U.K., should be manufactured to one of several Home Office specifications. The storage capacity of an aqualung cylinder is quoted in cubic feet: thus a cylinder quoted as having a capacity of 40 cubic feet would contain this amount of air (in compressed form) when filled to the appropriate pressure marked on the neck of the cylinder. This last statement is important, for cylinders (or 'bottles', as they are colloquially known) of set specifications have a maximum pressure that they can safely hold. For instance, given two cylinders of identical dimensions, number one having a maximum pressure of 1,000 p.s.i. and number two a maximum pressure of 2,000 p.s.i., the latter bottle would contain twice the amount of air than the former if both were filled to maximum pressure.

Aqualung cylinders should be handled with extreme care, for the pressures involved—usually at least 1,800 p.s.i.—make them potentially as dangerous as a bomb containing several pounds of dynamite. Rough handling is not the only factor that could goad a cylinder into exploding: poor maintenance can cause the interior walls to rust, reducing the thickness and with it the margin of safety; cylinders charged to pressures higher than the figure designated can suffer from fatigue on the metal walls; and yet another danger is the possibility of the cylinder being charged with a gas other than air. With regard to the latter, there is a colour code for gases stored in cylinders, that for air being grey, with black and white quartering at the valve end. All aqualung cylinders should be painted in this manner, and it is recommended that the words 'Breathing Air' be painted over in a contrasting colour. Cylinder care should be the first consideration of the free-diver, for this article, if maltreated, is a potential danger not only to the diver, but also to other people. A cylinder should never be stored with the valve tap open, for it is filled with comparatively dry air; if the tap were left open, moisture-laden air could enter and promote rust formation. A dented, deeply cut or abrased cylinder should be relegated to the scrap-heap.

There are a number of cylinders on the market and in use that have the dubious distinction of being ex-W.D. stock, particularly a small 25 cu. ft. model known as a Tadpole. Now these cylinders are old, and the metal often fatigued, constituting a danger to their owners and any-one else in their vicinity. Handling these ancient cylinders gently is no guarantee of safety: recently, a Tadpole exploded while reclining on the seat of a fortunately empty car. A standard procedure, when many of these ex-W.D. cylinders were rejected or retired, was to drill a small hole through the wall to render them un-usable; but in the 1950's, when aqualung equipment was at a premium, it was not unknown for misguided or unscrupulous individuals to weld those holes over. Little more need be said. Ensure that any cylinders you purchase come under a Home Office specification and possess a recent test certificate. Regulations require cylinders to be hydraulically tested every four years, but a safer plan is to test a new cylinder after three years and at two-year intervals thereafter.

The Harness

The harness should be judged as much for its comfort of fit as for its practical use. Free-diving equipment often has to be carried a considerable distance on foot in order to reach some diving sites, and an unbalanced, uncomfortable harness will chafe and exhaust its owner.

Although three (and even four) cylinders are sometimes worn by professionals and experimental groups, the single- and two-cylinder harnesses are the most popular among amateur free-divers. Should you contemplate purchasing a unit of two cylinders, consideration should be given to several harnesses on the market that are convertible, fitting either one or two bottles; you won't always require two cylinders, and a long walk carrying a heavy bulky twin-set is rather pointless if a short dive in shallow water is contemplated.

Apart from holding your cylinder(s) in place securely and comfortably, a good harness should possess efficient quick-release buckles and be easy to cast off while under water or while swimming on the surface. For should you ever need to jettison your aqualung, you will probably be in a hurry, tired, and exhausted.

The Air Supply

Too many free-divers are vague about the contents of their cylinders. A compressor should supply medically pure air; although air supplied from any depot of British Oxygen Gases (and the majority of commercial and club compressors) comes up to this standard, it is a fact that occasionally, perhaps owing to poor siting, air of dubious quality is supplied. Contamination can occur in several ways: exhaust fumes from cars, for example, can result in the induction of dangerous carbon monoxide; moisture-laden air—the result of an inadequate drying filter—can start rust formation on the interior walls; or, if a cylinder is filled too quickly, over-heated air is supplied, which, cooling rapidly, causes condensation to take place. The latter trouble can be eliminated by filling reasonably slowly and immersing the cylinders in water while they are being filled. Oil or dust can be particularly harmful to the lungs, and both can be introduced into the cylinder supply if the compressor is inadequately assembled or maintained.

The air endurance of a given cylinder is variable. This fluctuation is no fault of the equipment, but rather of the user. It is generally assumed that the average person consumes one cubic foot of air per minute on land, and this would seem to give us a good basis for calculation: a 40 cu. ft. cylinder would suffice a diver for 40 minutes at the surface; at 33 feet (double the pressure) the air would last for 20 minutes; at 99 feet (double again) it would be 10 minutes; etc. However, this rule, in practice, is at best only a very rough guide, for various factors have to be taken into consideration. A novice diver uses air at a much faster rate than an experienced diver, and even the latter's varies from day to day. A diver lazily browsing around will show an apparent economy of air as against his partner who is working furiously—in exactly the same way as a man walking uses less air than a man running (although in this case, the air supply is not limited). Then again, the average diver would not stay at a fixed depth, and the calculations involved—e.g. 5 minutes at 25 feet, 7 minutes at 31 feet, etc.—would necessitate the use of a computer.

It is logical that the free-diver should attempt to obtain maximum time under water from his air supply. To this end, it is foolhardy to practise breath-holding; not only is it dangerous, but it does not extend the duration of the air supply. Minimum air consumption is the result of a lazy, steady breathing rhythm: so avoid exertion, and, if swimming against a current over a rocky or seaweed bed, crawl along the bottom, pulling yourself along hand-over-hand. When swimming with a current, use your fins just enough to keep suspended, letting the water carry you along; but beware that you don't overdo it—you can drift a long way from boat or base without even realising.

V. Additional Equipment

The only really essential items of equipment for the free-diver are: mask, fins, demand valve, cylinder, and harness. But in practice there are other articles which, although not contributing directly to underwater swimming, are just as important if the diver is to have a safe, comfortable dive. Only the foolhardy would omit a snorkel tube from their basic equipment; it could be a live-saver if surfacing out of air with a long swim to the nearest landing-point. For similar reasons the life-jacket should be included on any dive. While protective clothing is of great importance in the cold climate of the British Isles, even in the sunny Mediterranean the diver requires some form of insulation if he is diving at even a moderate depth for a considerable length of time.

Principles and Selection of Protective Clothing

Apart from the aspect of comfort, divers in our part of the globe wear protective clothing all the year round, and for very practical reasons. Normal body temperature is 98·4 degrees Fahrenheit and a person immersed in water at a temperature considerably lower than this will suffer a loss of body heat, due to a gradual dissipation of this heat into the water. At very low temperatures warmth will be lost at a faster rate than that at which the body can replace it—then chilling commences. Chilling is liable to cause the diver to perform excessive movement in an

47

effort to keep warm, and while this is temporarily successful, it will accelerate the loss of body heat. A prolonged
immersion in cold water will befuddle the movements of
the hardiest individual, and a diver with numbed hands is
not capable of acting efficiently in an emergency; should
the need arise to jettison a weight-belt, or 'blow' a life-
jacket, it has to be done quickly, not fumbled with
chilled fingers. The ultimate result, after the slowing
down of both physical and mental reactions, is unconsciousness and drowning. A person swimming in near-
freezing water could expect to survive little more than
a quarter of an hour, but with full protective clothing,
this could be extended to a full hour without undue discomfort.

For all practical purposes there are two types of diving
suit, called appropriately enough, 'wet' and 'dry'; wet
suits are worn by the majority of the diving fraternity and,
by reason of popularity, merit first mention.

Wet suits are tailored from foam neoprene, approximately three-sixteenths of an inch thick. Identical in
construction to the well-known foam rubber, neoprene is
used as it has a greater resistance to sunlight, salt water,
and oil.

The wet suit should be a snug, yet comfortable fit. It
has no water-tight seals, for it functions by allowing a
little water to seep in to form a thin film of water between
the foam neoprene and the skin; the film of water soon
warms up to body temperature, and the minute air cells
in the foam material help to conserve this heat. Provided
the suit is snug enough to prevent the film of water from
circulating, and there are no spaces where pockets of
water can accumulate (these can cause trouble if situated
at the back, along the spine), then the coldest conditions
need cause no discomfort.

Wet suits can be obtained ready made in various sizes
—and prices—or in the form of a do-it-yourself kit; the

sheets of foam neoprene are supplied along with patterns, which are cut out from the sheets and stuck together with an impact adhesive. The seams are joined edge-to-edge, not overlapped, and form a secure bond that requires little maintenance. These kits probably provide the best value for money. Also, if the final fit is a little baggy, say at the knees, one can snip a slice of material out of each knee, then re-stick; but this procedure is far less attractive than a sleek ready-made model.

The latest innovation in wet suits is a nylon lining bonded to the inside. Apart from rendering the garment easier to put on, this has the additional advantage of making the suit almost tear-proof. Although a torn wet suit is no danger to the diver, the exposed portion of anatomy will prove a little uncomfortable in very cold water.

Wet suits are of fairly uniform design, but variations do occur, particularly in the jacket. This can have the hood attached or separate, and the system of fastening the front will be by heavy-duty zip or velcro fastener. The pullover type has no front opening at all—and the contortions that beset a diver trying to take off the latter, without assistance, have to be seen to be believed! The type of jacket ultimately selected is a matter of personal preference, there being nothing to choose between them for most practical purposes.

The buoyancy of the wet suit is an aspect that merits most careful attention. The composition of the material—millions of air pockets locked in neoprene—makes a wet suit very buoyant indeed: twenty-five pounds of lead on the weight belt are often needed when the suit is new. As the diver descends, the pockets of air are compressed by the pressure, and lose buoyancy. At this stage the diver will be over-weighted, and this can be a frightening experience for the beginner. It is difficult to avoid this difficulty—indeed, some experienced divers prefer to be

a little heavy when on the bottom; the important point is
to ensure that one is slightly buoyant when on the surface,
so that a long snorkel home would not prove too exhausting. An additional loss of buoyancy in a wet suit takes
place with age. After repeated dives, some of the air
pockets rupture, and one will find that less weight is
needed, often ending up with a quarter of the original
amount. Thus a constant check should be kept on
buoyancy, and weights dispensed with accordingly.

If the water is not too cold, a 'casual' wet suit can be
made up, consisting of a heavy woollen sweater, com-
binations and balaclava helmet. This attire will reduce
the flow of water next to the skin and, while not exactly a
picture of sartorial elegance, is very effective at moderate
temperatures. This ensemble usually requires no weight
belt and buoyancy is unaffected at any depth; in fact, the
diver may—depending on his equipment—be permanently heavy, in which case some buoyant article should
be worn that will compensate.

Dry suits are worn by less than 10 per cent of the diving
population, but there are circumstances in which a dry
suit holds a great advantage over its wet rival, despite the
immense popularity of the latter. The dry suit, as its name
implies, keeps the occupant from direct contact with the
water. Tailored from thin, flexible sheet rubber, usually
backed with fabric, and possessing water-tight seals at
the wrists, neck and head, this design allows the diver to
wear clothing underneath. In fact, underclothes are a
necessity, as sheet rubber is a very poor insulator against
cold.

The buoyancy problems of the dry suit are very
different from those of its wet counterpart. A dry suit
traps a large quantity of air in the cells of the undergarments. This should be vented off before diving, and is
achieved by holding open a wrist seal and submerging
the rest of the body, when the water pressure will drive

out the air through the open seal; if a tube is fitted for this purpose, the air can be sucked out. Once this procedure has been carried out, buoyancy under water will vary only a little.

A major characteristic of the dry suit is the effect of a 'squeeze'; at depth, the increased water pressure compresses any remaining air in the suit, and causes the rubber skin to grip the body tightly. Plate VIII (right). Increasing depth will render the suit very stiff—and the diver correspondingly immobile—while folds on the suit can pinch the skin and cause weals and blood blisters. Another disadvantage of the dry suit is the possibility of tearing. A small leak would cause only a little damp discomfort, but a severe tear will result in the woollen undergarments becoming saturated; this could be dangerous, as the diver will become rapidly overweight. If a large tear occurs on the upper portion of the suit, i.e. the back, it might become necessary to cut slits in the suit at the ankles, to allow the water a free flow. Water-logged trousers might prove an excessive burden even if the weight belt were jettisoned.

By now, the reason for the popularity of the wet suit is apparent with its freedom from 'squeeze', and ability to ignore tears. The big advantage of the dry suit lies in the principle of keeping the water from direct contact with the skin. A diver with full-face mask, dry suit, and gloves, is capable of diving in polluted waters without being exposed to the dangers of direct contact. As no evaporation chill takes place on the body, a dry suit is a more comfortable garment if he has to change in exposed, chilly conditions, or leave his suit on for some time after the dive has finished.

Protective clothing is worn to keep one warm and comfortable under water, so do not lessen its effectiveness by entering the water in a chilled condition. A vacuum flask of warm water can be emptied into the neck of a

wet suit—relieving the body of the chore of warming up
a film of cold water—while warmed undergarments will
ensure a comfortable dry suit dive. If the dry suit has a
venting tube, try a few exhalations into it at the end of a
cold dive.

It seems obvious that a chilled diver can do with a mug
of hot soup, tea or coffee at the end of his exertions, but
this item—along with a large towel—is often forgotten
in the excited preparations for an expedition.

Diving suits are made from tough materials, but careful
maintenance is necessary if they are to give of their best.
Post-dive procedure should include thorough rinsing,
particularly if the dive has been in salt water; drying;
repairs to suspect seams or tears; and a liberal sprinkling
of french chalk or talcum before the garments are packed
away.

Weight Belt

The positive buoyancy of protective clothing is such that
some form of ballast is required if the diver is to obtain
a neutral buoyancy under water and this is usually
achieved by wearing a weight belt. Lead weights are
added to the belt until the desired buoyancy is obtained.
One cannot be correctly weighted at all depths—the
compression of air in the suit makes buoyancy vary—
thus it is wise to ensure that one can float comfortably on
the surface when fully equipped. It may be a little harder
to swim the first ten feet or so down, but, should a diver
surface in distress, too much weight could prove fatal,
and until experience is gained, it is best to err on the side
of safety.

The function of a weight belt is to assist the diver to
descend; it follows that should he wish to dispense with
this facility he will want to do it quickly. A weight belt
should possess a reliable quick-release. An ordinary belt

strung with lumps of lead is a potentially lethal instrument. If a reasonable span of life is desired, a belt that can be released with a single sharp tug should be obtained; it should also be ensured that the release mechanism is large and easy to find. A short length of flimsy tape actuating an otherwise excellent quick release is of little use to the diver wearing thick gloves.

Practice releasing the weight belt. After the release, hold the belt away at arm's length before letting go. A belt released and allowed to drop freely could become snagged on another item of equipment—such as a knife strapped to the thigh—and there would be no time to fumble around. The weights should be easy to attach and remove, otherwise there is a tendency to leave excessive weight on 'until the next time'. With this attitude there might never be a next time!

Life-Jacket

An inflatable life-jacket is a non-essential item of diving equipment that, paradoxically, is universally considered indispensable. In other words, it is not wise to dive without one, and many a diver has had cause to be grateful for the presence of a life-jacket. Among the many uses for this article are: the diver who has surfaced, and is in difficulties; to help support another person in the same condition; assisting the diver to ascend, although this last procedure is a strictly emergency action. If losing consciousness, for instance, a life-jacket can whip a diver up at an uncontrollable speed during the last twenty feet and, apart from the possibility of cracking one's head against the bottom of a boat or other obstruction, this method of reaching the surface incurs the dangers of embolism and the bends.

Life-jackets on the market can be classified into two types by virtue of the emergency inflating mechanism.

The most popular (and cheapest) utilises a small cylinder charged with a compressed gas, carbon dioxide, and has a trigger device that is squeezed to actuate immediate inflation of the jacket. The cylinder is then of no further use and has to be replaced. This type should possess a mouth inflation tube, for you may be in no particular trouble, but desire a little extra buoyancy on the surface without going to the expense of expending the cylinder. A word of warning here, never fire the inflating mechanism while the jacket is already inflated, even partially, as this could cause the jacket to burst.

Although this jacket is the simplest to operate, and for this reason is the one most often used for training divers, there are a few points to note. The single charge of gas means that the jacket is at its most effective buoyancy on the surface of the water. When submerged, the jacket loses potential buoyancy owing to the compressive effects of water pressure. It will inflate fully if actuated on the surface, but at a depth of 33 feet firing the cylinder will result in a half-inflated jacket (as the water pressure has doubled) and the buoyancy will be halved. This effect is progressive. The deeper the diver, the less potential buoyancy the jacket has, until, at a specific depth, varying with the individual, the jacket could be ineffective as a 'lift'.

The second type of life-jacket utilises a cylinder of compressed air, which can be re-charged from any compressor or the diver's own air tanks. The only jacket of this type available at the time of writing is the French Fenzy; but this description only applies to that article.

Inflation can be controlled by turning a valve, and maximum inflation (buoyancy) can be achieved at any depth the diver is likely to reach. A relief valve releases expanding air on the upward journey, to prevent bursting. This gives, in effect, a continuously inflated jacket, and lifts the diver to the surface at a considerable speed.

Although an obviously useful function to the diver in dire straits, a fast rate of ascent is fraught, as mentioned before, with the dangers of embolism and the bends. This jacket is an item of equipment for the experienced diver, not the novice. The fact that the diver can now adjust his buoyancy while under water probably makes this type the jacket of the future. But careful tuition, and experience, is required before it can be worn safely.

The usual colour of a life-jacket is orange, for easy identification. The material, rubber-proofed fabric, should be checked for perforations before each dive. After use, rinse the jacket with fresh water, ensure that no water has entered (through the mouth inflation tube perhaps), dry thoroughly, dust with french chalk, and pack carefully away from sharp objects. The emergency inflating device should be frequently inspected for corrosion.

Ancillary Equipment

Having obtained the essential equipment relating to function and safety, the diver is confronted with a bewildering variety of instruments and mechanisms that possess varying degrees of utility. Their usefulness will depend upon the individual—the diver working in conditions that might cause him to become ensnared in ropes or cables will consider a knife essential, while the diver performing feats that require decompression would consider a good watch more useful.

Knife

A knife is the most popular 'extra', and serves many purposes. It will be used for prising, chopping, sawing, and, of course, cutting! It follows that it should conform to a general pattern of construction, as some of the knives on the market were never manufactured with underwater work in mind. The floating varieties have their uses, but mainly for the boat owner or snorkeling spear-fisherman. A diver's knife should be of robust construction: one that could be used, if necessary, as a lever. One edge should be serrated, and is used for cutting through heavy rope or cable; the other edge will possess a plain cutting surface. A stainless steel blade requires less maintenance than hardened steel—the latter will rust if not protected with grease. The handle should be large enough to grasp firmly while wearing bulky foam-neoprene gloves, with a non-slip surface and a guard large enough to prevent the hand from slipping on to the blade.

The sheath needs to be of efficient design. Metal, fibreglass, or heavy plastic are better than leather or fabric, which are of little use. Metal sheaths usually hold the blade by means of a strong spring affixed to the inside, and while this method has survived the test of time, the blade can, in certain circumstances, be dragged out accidentally. A short length of nylon line should eliminate the danger of losing the knife if this happens. Plastic sheaths often secure the knife with a small clip around the handle, or a short length of elastic. This is fine if the diver is not wearing thick gloves, when it can become difficult to manipulate the clip or piece of elastic. The position of the knife is one of individual preference. If worn at the waist, do not secure it to the weight belt, as this item might be jettisoned in an emergency. Many divers strap the sheath to the thigh, where at least it is unencumbered by the equipment covering the torso.

Compass

The compass is indispensable for direction finding, or compiling a detailed search or survey. Under water, the sense of direction can deteriorate rapidly, and it is advisable that the diver, particularly when at sea, should know where the shore, or boat, lies.

The popular type of compass is of little use under water—it will fill with water or implode—thus it is essential that a compass for underwater use be of the liquid filled type. Apart from this consideration, the dial of a liquid-filled compass is more steady than most of the jerky, air-spaced variety. All markings should have a good coating of luminous paint, to enable readings to be taken in the dim light often encountered under water.

Leather or plastic is usually used for the strap. If possible, remove this and replace with heavy-gauge elastic webbing or an expanding bracelet. This will ensure that the compass fits the wrist snugly at any depth, as the solid strap will fit well on the surface, but hang loose at depth, when the water pressure compresses the suit.

Depth Gauge

Every diver likes to know the maximum depth of his dive—whether it has been a twenty-foot 'paddle' or a really deep one. Experienced divers often claim that they can accurately estimate their current depth; but these boasts seldom stand up in practice, for one aspect of human estimation is its variability. There are times, such as whilst decompressing, when a method of ascertaining depth is essential. This is where the depth gauge comes in. This instrument is rarely 100 per cent accurate, but is usually adequate for diving; it is balanced for use in sea water. When diving in fresh water, or above or below sea level, slight inaccuracies will be obtained owing to the difference in density of fresh water and/or the change in atmospheric pressure. The most expensive depth gauge is not always the best or most reliable, and if dives deeper than 40 feet are not contemplated, and you are careful when using it, the capillary depth gauge is probably the best value. This consists of a glass or Perspex tube, open at one end and closed at the other. On immersion, water enters the tube and compresses the trapped air; the greater the depth, the greater the penetration of water. Readings are then taken from the air-water demarcation line in the same manner as a thermometer. Capillary gauges need care in use. Never jump into the water when wearing one, as this causes a series of bubbles to accumulate in the tube. As the gauge enters the water, ensure that the open end is pointing down into it; this will prevent a small bubble of air escaping and ruining your readings. Also ensure that there are no obstructions in the tube—even a drop of water can cause wide error.

The other types of gauge—Bourdon tube and diaphragm system—are read off the dial by a sweep hand or needle. The cheaper models never seem to function well until a depth of around 50 feet is reached (the opposite of the capillary), but are more accurate below this depth.

Some of the more expensive variety have a maximum-depth-reached indicator: these can be used on a sounding line for a pre-dive check.

Watch

A watch has many fields of application under water. It is essential for dives requiring decompression, or complicated navigational exercises—then again, you may merely want to know the time.

The cheapest underwater timepiece is obtained by enclosing an ordinary watch in a waterproof housing, but more popular is the watch designed for use under water. Prices vary, but technology in this field has advanced to the degree where most makes are reliable. When selecting a watch for diving make sure it is luminous (light can get deceptively dim under water): a sweep second hand is necessary for navigation purposes, and a rotating bezel for recording the start of the dive or decompression stop.

Torch

A torch is indispensable for browsing around wrecks, exploring nooks and crannies in the rock face, and night diving. In fresh water an ordinary household torch will function well even when flooded, but the same procedure in sea water will, owing to the short-circuiting action of salt water on electricity, result in no usable light—also, if your reflector is plated this will strip off in seconds.

In the circumstances where artificial lighting is needed, something reliable is essential. There are several solid diving torches on the market, so try to afford an instrument designed for the job. The all-rubber torch is usually designed to be waterproof, not subject to pressure, but if the work is not too important or dangerous (such as night diving), then this type can be used after a little doctoring with sealing compound.

Writing Under Water

For the purpose of recording or communicating under water, some form of writing material is often required. A writing slate for underwater use can be purchased, but it is really better to make your own, as the article can then be tailored to your requirements. An ordinary slate or sandpapered white plastic can be used, but if you only have clear plastic available, roughen one side and paint the other side white. In all cases the writing instrument is an ordinary lead pencil, which should be attached to the slate or plastic with a short length of elastic or a clip.

Thermometer

Any ordinary thermometer can be used under water, and it is not necessary to pay a high price. If only general information is required, then the lower price range will provide an adequate instrument. If the records are needed for scientific purposes, then a thermometer such as the type used for colour photography—guaranteed plus or minus not more than half a degree—is probably the best value. The thermometer is usually mounted on the edge of the writing-tablet, which affords it some protection and makes it convenient for recording.

VI. Free-Diving Techniques

PART ONE—BASIC TECHNIQUES

The Standard Required

Local conditions, and the availability of suitable equipment, create differing approaches to technique and training in various parts of the world. However, there is one cardinal rule that is universally approved by amateur free-divers: Never Dive Alone. Disregarding this maxim has no doubt accounted for many deaths and, strangely, the application of this rule has also caused fatalities for it is inadequately worded, despite its world-wide acceptance. A more accurate wording would read: Never Dive Without An Adequate Partner. An underwater companion who is always missing when needed, or is poorly trained, is not a suitable person to whom to entrust your life—and that is what it amounts to. It takes little to achieve a reasonable standard of proficiency: a sturdy finning action; competence in mask and hose clearing; practical knowledge of emergency procedures, thorough familiarity with free-diving equipment and its dangers are all that is required.

Training

Your aqualung lessons should be carried out under the expert eye of a qualified instructor, but there are several points that we can discuss in advance, so that you can present yourself suitably primed.

The first stage of instruction will be on the practical aspects of the aqualung. Before you enter the water, a check should be made to ensure that the cylinder is adequately filled, and the demand valve is functioning correctly. The first check is on the cylinder valve washer. Examine this to see that it is not pitted, cut, or damaged in any other way. Next attach the demand valve to the cylinder valve: the connection should be tightened by hand—never with a spanner or similar tool. The contents of the cylinder are checked with the pressure gauge. Lay the fitted aqualung down and turn the glass fronted face of the pressure gauge *away* from you, then turn the cylinder valve on. The set should be left in this position for a full five minutes before the gauge is picked up and the contents read. There is, of course, a reason for this sequence. Should there be a fault in the pressure-gauge seals, it is sometimes possible for air to leak into the space between the face and glass front, causing it to explode after three or four minutes, or sometimes almost immediately. Although the possibility of this happening is extremely remote, it is obviously pointless to take chances for the sake of a few minutes. Having assured yourself of an adequate air supply, turn the cylinder valve off, and watch the gauge carefully. The needle should remain firm at maximum pressure. If it drops steadily, there is a high-pressure leak—this could be at the cylinder valve washer connection, the gauge tube, or the demand valve. Should the needle fail to drop, place the mouthpiece in your mouth and suck out the available air. If you continue to inhale a little air after the gauge needle has dropped to zero, a low-pressure leak is indicated, probably at the point where the air-hose joins the mouthpiece or demand valve.

Having assured yourself of the condition of your equipment, your first test will probably be the fitting on of aqualung, mask and fins while under water. This will

consist of sinking your equipment, with the aid of a
weight belt, diving down (using a neat jack-knife dive),
fitting the mouthpiece, laying the weight belt over your
legs (to prevent floating to the surface), adjusting the
harness, clearing the mask, fitting fins, weight belt and
snorkel, and returning to the surface. The sting will be
taken out of this exercise if you have been practising
fitting fins, mask and snorkel on a single breath, as mentioned in Chapter II.

Other exercises, and tests, will consist of swimming
along the bottom of the pool, with your mask blacked
out to check on any possible claustrophobic tendencies
and sharing an aqualung under water, which will increase
your confidence and breathing rhythm. The exercises
and tests demanded by club or school are designed to
lead you into free-diving with confidence, efficiency, and
safety. Don't try to evade them, for maximum enjoyment
comes with confidence in one's ability.

A Typical Dive

On the assumption that nothing teaches as well as
practical experience, let us go through the actual motions
in an imaginary dive, from the start to finish. The location is a sandy beach set in a sheltered bay. It will be a
shore dive, as no boat is available, and cover will be
provided by snorkel divers. You are standing on the
beach, resplendent in swimming costume, surrounded by
neatly laid out diving equipment.

First clear up the jobs you can perform before you
climb into your bulky suit. You will have tested your
cylinder for its contents long before you started out, so
now check the valve washer and replace if necessary.
Then open the cylinder valve for a brief second, to clear
the orifice of any sand or moisture that may have
accumulated. Next examine the demand valve filter for

any similar accumulations, and connect the demand valve to the cylinder. Turn the pressure gauge face so that it is pointing away from you (or anyone else), and open the cylinder valve. While waiting for the five-minute safety period to elapse, examine your life-jacket for possible tears or punctures. If the emergency inflation cylinder is of the compressed air type—such as a Fenzy—ensure that it has been filled. This done, return to your aqualung unit, close the cylinder valve, and check for contents and high- or low-pressure leaks. The test for a low-pressure leak will also enable you to 'taste' the air in case some dangerous fumes should have entered during filling. After each inhalation through the mouthpiece, exhale slowly through the nose. This test will not enable you to assess positively whether the air is pure, but it is sometimes possible to detect excessively 'oily' air, or carbon monoxide fumes given off by a petrol engine.

After carefully donning your protective suit—wet or dry—it is important to observe certain priorities in fitting the equipment. It will be necessary to fit either the aqualung or life-jacket on first—the correct sequence depending upon the particular construction of each. A life-jacket should not be covered by harness straps but should be inflatable over them. When harness straps cross the chest, ensure that the life-jacket holding-tapes are secure underneath them. More simply, make sure that you can jettison your aqualung while leaving the life-jacket in position. Last of all comes the weight belt. This item is placed over all other equipment, dropping freely when the quick-release is pulled. This may seem obvious, but it is surprising how many free-divers enter the water with their weight belt strapped *underneath* their aqualung harness, and quite impossible to release in a hurry.

Bring your mouthpiece into position just under your

chin, place the mask on your forehead, snorkel in place, and fit auxiliary items such as your watch, depth gauge, etc. The question of fins depends upon the distance from kitting-up to the point of entry. If a fairly long walk is necessary, carry the fins and fit at the water's edge, but in this case as you are on the beach with immediate access to the water, you would have fitted fins while donning the suit. On arrival at the water's edge, spit in your mask and rinse to prevent misting, and get someone to turn on your air. Meanwhile the instructor, or dive leader, will be giving his orders. Under water, you are to swim slightly behind him, on his right. The dive will take place along a rocky ridge about 200 yards out—to save air the journey out will be made on snorkel. The final check is on weight—you don't want to be heavy while swimming on the surface—and you are away.

As you snorkel out, mask buried in the water, the sea-bed unfolds its mysterious landscape. Fronds of seaweed sway rhythmically in the mild wave surge and a purple, translucent jelly-fish drifts lazily along. The bottom slopes gently away, and visibility is reduced to an opaque blue-green, when suddenly a rock points its finger through the green velvet fog. The location has been reached. Change over from snorkel to aqualung. The dive leader tenders the O.K. sign, which is returned all round. A neat jack-knife dive and you are, for a while, in a world of fantasy.

About 10 feet down, the water pressure becomes apparent on your ears: a gentle clearing motion and you are on your way down again. Down to 35 feet, then the bottom, and you become conscious of a little water in your mouthpiece. The method of eliminating this excess depends upon the type of demand valve. With a twin-hose model, turn sideways so that the exhaust hose (sometimes on the right, but usually on the left: this point should be checked, and noted before you submerge) is on the bottom, or sea-bed side, and the inlet hose towards the surface. Blow into the mouthpiece. Water in a single-hose mouthpiece requires a different procedure. The centre of the mouthpiece contains a 'purging' button—pressing this activates the diaphragm and causes a flush of air. Of course, you will be well drilled in these exercises before you go on a dive.

A further interchange of O.K. signs, and you take off, keeping carefully on the designated side of the leader. Now you can look around. At your approach, a tiny hermit crab scuttles across the sandy bottom and, leaping into a whelk shell several sizes too small, frantically claws the shell like a fat woman trying to struggle into a steel corset! A rocky outcrop sporting strap-like seaweed, comes into view, and also a small colony of that colourful marine 'hedgehog', the sea urchin. The sand around is dotted with intricately whorled piles of sand—the deposits of the lug-worm. You look up—the exhaust valves of your companions are emitting a silver plume of bubbles that disappear gently into the silver-green of the surface. Now the dive leader stops, and solemnly takes hold of your pressure gauge. With a start, you remember that you were supposed to inform him when the pressure dropped to 60 atmospheres, then 30. The reading is now 35. Luckily you can't hear him muttering as he sets his compass sights for shore. The vegetation becomes more prolific as the floor slopes gently upwards. You concentrate on breathing steadily, taking care not to inhale deeply.

Back on shore, however tired, don't just throw your aqualung unit on the beach. Carefully remove the demand valve from the cylinder, and pack each neatly away, safe from gritty particles, along with the life-jacket.

The above dive, although described as typical, could, of course, have had several different permutations. A boat would have necessitated a vertical ascent, the visibility could have been very poor, and an emergency could have occurred.

On the Surface

It cannot be repeated too many times: a free-diver, laden with equipment, is most vulnerable when on the surface, and probably out of air. There are several points that should be borne in mind—or practised—long before a long snorkel home in full kit is undertaken.

Always check that you are slightly buoyant on the surface before you submerge. In case of error, you can always fall back on your weight belt quick-release, but don't wait until you are half-drowned before groping for the buckle. A common cause of difficulty is the change-over from aqualung to snorkel, particularly in choppy water. You should run through the change-over, in training, until the procedure becomes second nature. It is common practice, among experienced divers, who use a life-jacket possessing a mouthpiece, to partially inflate the jacket before commencing a long snorkel. This again is a procedure with which you should be thoroughly familiar before attempting it on a dive.

A problem often mentioned is whether, if in difficulty on the surface, to inflate the life-jacket first, or release the weight belt. Of course if in acute difficulty, the quickest solution is the best, and this means the life-jacket—problems can arise with snagged or awkward belts. However, if you are merely very tired, and in no acute distress, an inflated life-jacket can cause additional drag, especially going against a current, and in these circumstances the weight belt could best be released.

The weight of a cylinder worn 'riding high' can tend to push down on a snorkelling free-diver. If conditions permit, swimming on the back will result in the cylinder and valve being immersed, and the swim back made a little easier.

The Ascent

The normal ascent poses few problems. Steady, regular breathing, with a shallow intake and positive exhalation, and a speed that does not exceed that of the smallest exhaust bubbles will ensure a safe ascent. But an emergency ascent? There are two methods of ascent in an emergency—free and assisted—both fraught with danger, and both requiring detailed knowledge—not only practice—of the procedures.

In a free ascent, as its name implies, the diver, out of air, ascends rapidly on his own. The danger of surfacing rapidly (apart from the 'bends') is the possibility of damaging the lungs due to the expansion of what air they contained at the commencement of the ascent. The procedure, should a free ascent be forced upon you, is to breath out all the way up, while trying to keep calm (this last is almost impossible of course, but panic consumes precious oxygen very quickly). It must be emphasised that a free ascent should *not* be practised in training, for the dangers inherent in any free ascent more than offset the knowledge gained.

However, we can safely simulate the efforts in the swimming-pool, without an aqualung. Clad in mask and fins, retire to the deep end. Take a deep breath, jack-knife to the bottom, and swim towards the shallow end exhaling gently through the mouth continuously. The distance covered under water should not exceed 25 yards, and ask someone to keep an eye on you whilst doing so.

A correct assisted ascent is described as follows. A diver's air supply fails. He attracts his partner's attention, and signals, indicating that he requires air. His partner swims close to him, keeping slightly below him, passing up his mouthpiece. The victim has very little water to clear from the mouthpiece, for the fact that the mouthpiece has been offered upwards ensures that the air is flushing through. Then, in turn, each diver takes two breaths before returning the mouthpiece. When a regular breathing pattern is established they ascend steadily, each holding the other firmly with his free hand.

On paper, of course, this method seems very workable. But in practice it requires intensive training in the swimming-pool, *never* at depths greater than 25 feet. It is relatively easy to 'share' while both of you are static, but when moving, complications can occur. Should one or both divers be poorly trained in this exercise, and an attempt at an assisted ascent—emergency or otherwise—from depth, be attempted, an error is probable, placing both of them in danger.

Hand Signals

Accurate basic communications between divers, and from diver to lookout, is essential for several reasons. It ensures safer diving and prevents wasting time with confusing charades. The signals (Fig. 4) should be kept to simple, easy-to-read actions or poses.

There is no international code of underwater and surface hand signals, as various countries differ in certain aspects, but the following selection are in general use throughout most of the diving world, and recognised by most of the major organisations.

You, me or *that*. With the index finger (or complete hand if wearing mittens) the diver points to himself, another diver, or a specific object, and indicates the person or object to which the following signals refer.

Are you all right?/All is well. The thumb and index

finger form a circle as illustrated, (Fig. 4a). and can be used as a question or reply.

Stop. The hand is opened and the palm held outwards, facing the receiver of the command. The signal is identical to that used by policemen on point duty.

Go up/I am going up. The fist is clenched, with the thumb extending upwards to the surface (Fig. 4c). This signal will usually be preceded by another, such as *you*, or *stop*.

Go Down/I am going down. The same as the last signal except that the fist is inverted, with the thumb pointing down.

I have 30 ats. left in my cylinder/I am on reserve. The fist is clenched, and held at eye level, on the right-hand side of the mask with the finger knuckles facing the recipient of the signal (Fig. 4d).

Distress. The fist is waved, in a semi-circle, from shoulder to shoulder, passing the front of the mask with each action (Fig. 4b). It indicates that immediate assistance is required. *Danger*. The hand is drawn across the front of the neck, in a cut-throat movement.

The diver or snorkel cover on the surface will need to indicate the situation regularly to the lookout. There are two basic signals here.

Are you all right?/We are all right. The arm is thrust straight up, with the thumb and index finger in the *all is well* position (Fig. 4e.). Used as a question or reply.

Distress, come and get me or (from the lookout to diver), *come in immediately*. The arm is outstretched, and waved from side to side in a semi-circle (Fig. 4f).

Underwater Navigation

Visibility in Britsh waters will rarely exceed 20 feet, and the average will probably be in the region of 8 feet. The free-diver is therefore unable to use some of the more useful directional aids such as fixing sights on a distant

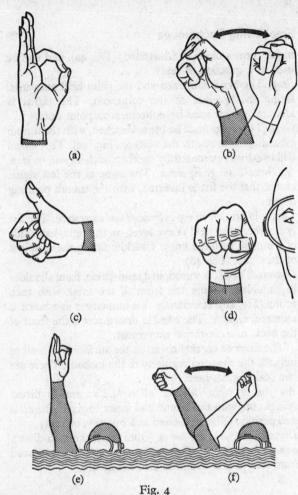

Fig. 4

(a) Are you all right?/All is well.

(b) Distress.

(c) Go up/I am going up (invert for: Go down/I am going down).

(d) I have only 30 ats. left in my cylinder/I am on reserve.

(e) (surface) Are you all right?/We are all right.

(f) (surface) Distress, come and get me/Come in immediately.

object, or the direction of the sun. But as it is important that the diver should know the direction of the shore or boat, for functional safety requirements, he has to adapt remaining aids to comply with underwater conditions.

Primitive navigation can be carried out by the observation of directional aids. A steady current, for instance, will include much free-moving sediment that can be easily seen. The direction of the current can be fixed at the surface, giving an experienced free-diver a rough approximation of his position under water at all times. Using this method, tide tables should be charted in advance, for it is of little use if local currents should be turning, or variable. Sand ripples can also give a rule-of-thumb directional guide for the free-diver, as they will often run in the same direction for considerable distances. The usual method of swimming a course in a straight line is by sighting of objects in line. Three objects are sighted, say a large pebble near by, a rock in the middle distance, and a patch of seaweed at the limit of vision. Ensuring that these items are in fact, in line, the diver swims from pebble to rock, then proceeds to look for another object in line beyond the patch of weed, and so on. If three objects are kept continually sighted it is possible to swim a remarkably straight path. For diving on a flat, sandy, featureless bottom, you should have prepared a length of wood or metal (twelve inches of broom handle is excellent) which is trailed by hand along the bottom as you swim out, creating a narrow groove that will guide you unerringly back to your point of entry.

A good liquid-filled compass is essential for detailed navigation and search procedure providing its drawbacks are recognized, and studied. Being magnetic, a compass is badly affected by metal objects in the vicinity, and the free-diver is well laden with metal—steel cylinder, demand valve, knife, etc. Provided the compass is always read from the same position, these errors will remain constant and can for general purposes be ignored. A more serious threat comes from objects that do not retain the same position and distance, such as your companion's equipment, the anchor chain, or a wreck. An important point to remember is that a compass cannot take a bearing on an object—it can only give you a bearing in the

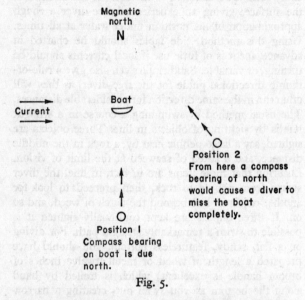

Fig. 5.

line of which your object lies. For instance, in our diagram (Fig. 5) the diver in position 1 could find his way back to the boat by following his compass reading of direct North. Should, however, the current carry him downstream to position 2, we can see that by following his compass reading of North, he will miss the boat by a considerable margin. Calculations to compensate for conditions such as this can only, at best, be a guess, although experience and training can produce remarkable accuracy. Bad navigation can produce dangerous situations, so if there is the slightest doubt in your mind as to your position, surface immediately and check your bearings. In any case this should be done when your air supply falls to half pressure, and again when low, to ensure that you can make it back to base under water, without the necessity of a long, tiring snorkel back.

PART TWO—ADVANCED DIVING

Roped Diving

As the title suggests, a free-diver is—subject to the limitations of time imposed by his air supply—un-encumbered by attachments to the surface. Occasions arise, however, when safety and functional efficiency necessitate a positive connection to the surface. Among the advantages of a roped dive are: that basic signals can be interchanged between diver and surface; that the diver can be hauled to the surface should circumstances warrant it; that should the diver become entangled with an obstruction, the standby diver can locate him immediately and that in conditions of zero visibility and light, the diver can locate his point of entry by returning along the rope, or signalling to be pulled up.

In conditions that indicate roped connections, a companion diver is sometimes an encumbrance. Low-visibility diving is best carried out by an experienced solo diver, in partnership with a surface tender who is well versed in this type of work. Where a companion is a possible asset—under ice, for instance—the more experienced diver is roped to a surface line, and attached to his partner by a short wrist-to-wrist line.

Because of the dangers of entanglement with one's

own line, a sturdy, sharp knife should be carried by all divers (including the standby) participating in roped diving. The knife should be secured to the sheath or knife belt (never to the weight belt—see Chapter V) by a short length of nylon cord or strong elastic tape.

The surface line should be securely attached to the diver, in a position clear of equipment such as mask, demand valve, hose, etc., and any quick-release buckles. The line can be secured around the diver's waist, before he dons his aqualung, or it can be fastened to the aqua-lung harness. Lead the rope, from its securing position at the back, under the armpit of the signalling arm, along the forearm, and hold it with two turns around the hand. *Never* secure it by turns around the forearm or wrists.

Most of the advantages of roped diving—particularly in low visibility—are lost unless both diver and surface tender are well practised. Signalling with a surface line should be on the agenda during pool training. Signals cannot be transmitted along a loose line. At all times the line should be as taut as comfort will allow, so that both tender and diver can 'feel' one another. It is preferable that the surface tender also be an experienced diver: this qualification will ensure that the tender can appreciate fully the possible difficulties of the submerged diver.

The surface line should be less than half an inch in diameter, but thick enough to grasp firmly, and capable of supporting a dead weight in excess of 500 pounds.

Low Visibility

The cause of low visibility can be suspended sediment, poor light, or both. In any case, it is usually better for the diver(s) to be roped to a surface tender. The limitations of visibility that necessitate a surface line will obviously vary with the experience of the diver(s). In general, when visibility is less than two feet, a diver is better off diving alone with a surface line. If visibility exceeds two feet, diving can be carried out in pairs, the more experienced diver secured to a surface line, and both attached by a short wrist-to-wrist line. As the dangers of diving in water of low visibility include entanglement with submerged items such as rope and wire, branches of felled trees, etc., essential equipment should include a knife and torch. A check on any claustrophobic tendencies can be carried out in a swimming-pool, with a fully blacked-out mask.

Under water, don't fin along in a hurry when vision is nil. Feel your way along slowly, to ensure that you do not swim into a submerged barrel, drum, or tank. Also, surface slowly and carefully, with one hand extended upwards, otherwise there is a possibility of cracking your head against a boat, jetty, or a swimming or floating article.

Diving at Night

Diving at night attracts an ever-growing band of enthusiasts. The underwater world is never exactly noisy, but at night the silence becomes positively eerie. Divers' torches cut silver tunnels through black velvet water, and colours appear brighter, and more intense in the light of a good torch.

It must be pointed out that much normal diving procedure is inapplicable to night diving. Signals obviously suffer. On the surface, the lookout can only be communicated with by a pre-arranged set of Morse-type torch signals. Keep these signals short and simple to avoid mishaps. All that are basically needed are: 1. *I am (we are) O.K.*; 2. *I am (we are) in distress*. From personal experience the writer has evolved the following signals: 1. *O.K.* Two short flashes, repeated several times; 2. *Distress.* A continual beam. The repetition of signal 1 is in case the lookout should miss the first, while a continual beam will assist the rescuers in locating the distressed diver(s).

Under water, the divers should keep strictly to pre-arranged pairs, and each diver should keep in close contact with his partner, for if your companion gets into trouble and his light fails, it will be almost impossible to find him.

The location of a night dive is of paramount importance. In lakes and similar areas, things will, with luck, go according to plan. But at sea a close check should be kept on tide tables. A headland jutting out to sea is a potentially dangerous hazard in daylight: at night a diver could be swept well away before an alarm is raised. The best type of sea location would seem to be a sheltered bay when tides are at neaps.

It would not be superfluous to take a spare torch under water, as a torch always seems to expire when most needed. And the underwater world can be a frightening place if you are suddenly plunged into darkness. Ensure that the torch you take under is adequately constructed for underwater use, and has been tested on several daylight dives. A knife should also be placed on the essential list.

Diving Under Ice

It is dubious whether diving under ice has as great a visual attraction as night diving. Nevertheless this form of sub-aquatic activity has its devotees—they can be seen at the bar, always drinking double brandies, and sporting purple, balloon-sized goose-pimples.

Whatever the thickness of the ice, diving should always be carried out in conjunction with a surface line, and the line should not in any circumstances be paid out more than 25 feet if the dive is horizontal, i.e. away from the entry hole. If the dive is vertical, i.e. straight down-and-up, on a weighted shot line, the line securing the lead diver might be paid out farther than 25 feet if the diver is experienced.

The necessity of a life-jacket is debatable. More life-jackets are inflated unnecessarily, in a moment of panic, than are inflated in genuine emergency. While this is no great danger in normal conditions, under ice the diver, ascending the last 10 feet at a considerable speed could, upon contact with the ice, injure himself or dislodge some essential equipment. The best solution would seem to be to acquire a standard of at least second-class B.S-A.C. before venturing under ice, after which a life-jacket could be worn with reasonable assurance.

Fast-moving Rivers

Diving in swift, clear, river current can provide an exhilarating activity for well-trained and experienced divers.

Ropes are a dubious advantage, as the danger of a diver tumbling along, swept in the current, becoming entangled and perhaps, again, displacing some essential equipment is possible.

In these conditions it is a good policy to swim against the current. This serves two purposes: avoiding the current getting a 'grip' on you, and perhaps sweeping you against some rocks; also the mud churned up by your fins will be carried downstream, not along your line of vision.

Cave Diving

There is enough to see and experience under water to last a lifetime, without venturing into the dangers of cave diving. Pot-holing on land requires substantial skill, training, and experience. Under water far more is required of all three, and in addition there is absolutely no margin of error. Scientific expeditions sometimes find it necessary to explore caves under water, but the only advice on cave diving that can safely be given to the amateur, pleasure-liking free-diver is—*don't*.

The Towing Sledge or Aquaplane

The towing sledge is really a cross between a surf-board, water-skis, and a sledge. In practice a board of marine plywood, approximately 6 feet long and 3 feet wide is towed by the boat, with a free-diver reclining on its uppermost surface. The board can ascend and descend via manually operated planing flaps, and sometimes a windscreen is built on to protect the diver from the self-imposed 'current'.

This sledge is ideal for searching large areas of clear water quickly. The lack of exertion enables the diver to extend his air supply and, consequently, his time under water. None the less, the aquaplane is no vehicle for the novice diver. The 'aquaplaner' has a considerable force of water opposing him, and the possibility of this force dislodging his mask is always present. Also, the aquaplane is capable of ascending more steeply than is apparent, with the accompanying danger of an embolism, when the planing flaps are in the 'up' position, regulate breathing to half breaths. When ascending in order to surface, breathe out as if in a free ascent, unless a gradual upward plane can be accurately gauged.

Never use the aquaplane when visibility is poor as there is always the danger of collision with some underwater object. The passenger should never be tied or in any other way secured to the aquaplane: the mere act of releasing his grip should be enough to release him from the board.

The Underwater Scooter

Much relating to the aquaplane also applies to the underwater scooter. The scooter is an electric propulsion device for towing a free-diver either on the surface or at depth. It has advantages over the aquaplane in that the speed can be regulated and there is no dependence upon a surface unit or connection.

For the mechanically minded, here is a brief description of one such scooter on the market. The 'Squid', manufactured by North End Works, is an underwater electric propulsion unit. The overall length is 3 feet 6 inches. It weighs 70 pounds with batteries, although buoyancy under water can be adjusted to near zero, or eliminated by trimming weights. Power is supplied by two 12-volt 25–ampere-hour non-spill batteries. Top speed is about 2 m.p.h., and the maximum running time is nearly two hours. However, if the batteries are reconnected to give 6 volts, the unit will run all day at better than average swimming speed. The trigger-operated switch, when released, cuts off the motor but can be locked in the 'on' position. The body is made of polyester resin and fibreglass, with steel end covers electro-galvanized, passivated and painted.

Wrecks

Diving on wrecks is an activity of many facets, such as the thrill of exploring a sunken vessel, the dangers lurking in such exploration, and lastly the legal aspect. The last item is of great importance, because there is always the temptation to recover objects from a wreck and take them home, or to the clubhouse, as souvenirs.

Every wreck, or portion of it, has a legal owner who is entitled to every part of the wreck, including the cargo. Any person who removes part of a wreck with the

Fig. 6. Artist's impression of the North End 'Squid'.

intention of depriving the legal owner permanently of possession, is committing an offence. The punishment, if one is convicted of such an offence, includes imprisonment for an impressive number of years. The consent of the owner, who can usually be traced through Lloyds' shipping list, should be obtained before anything is removed.

Of course, there is nothing to prevent you sight-seeing, and wreck hunting and diving lays claim to the largest group of enthusiasts in any branch of underwater activity. Wrecks usually exhibit prolific marine growths, and serve as a home for many fish. A knowledge of the history of a sunken vessel, including the events leading to the disaster, can make the dive that much more interesting. If the wreck is indicated on an Admiralty Chart, the Hydrographic Department can sometimes give you some details, for a small fee. When the name, and year of sinking, have been ascertained, the Shipping Editor of Lloyds can probably fill in the rest of the picture—again for a fee.

It should be remembered that wrecks are potentially unstable. There can be little or no warning should they move, or a section capsize. For this reason, it is not wise to enter a wreck. A good torch is essential when looking over most wrecks, as there will be many dark nooks and crannies to peer into. Don't thrust your hands into these cavities—a conger or crab might take exception! Rusting metal parts will, in time, erode to the thickness of a knife edge, and there is plenty of metal in most wrecks, so be careful when you come into actual contact or you might surface with some nasty gashes.

VII. At Sea and Inland

PART ONE—AT SEA

Dive Planning and Procedure

Whatever the cause, it is a fact that, apart from choosing the general location and date, diving excursions are often very inadequately planned nowadays. An approach such as this will rarely enable the participants to obtain the maximum enjoyment from the dive—not to mention the safety element—and, as a result, enthusiasm can soon pall.

An emergency is the time when the real value of advance planning is shown. Thus the first items of information to obtain are the addresses and telephone numbers of the nearest doctor, hospital, coastguard, and recompression chamber. The first two will probably be easier to obtain on arrival at the diving location, but the latter pair should be obtained in advance.

A nautical chart of the area is indispensable to any well-planned diving expedition. Research on coastal features, depths, tides, wrecks, restricted or dangerous areas, quality of the bottom, etc., can be carried out in advance, saving valuable time. Having obtained the chart, mark off potentially interesting sites. Reefs and rocky outcrops usually prove interesting, often abounding in fish life and lost anchors. Check any wrecks: if the chart is an Admiralty publication, the Hydrographic Department—for a small fee—can sometimes give you information on a marked wreck and the knowledge obtained can make the dive that much more interesting.

The Admiralty publish an annual catalogue of their nautical charts. Any study of Admiralty charts requires a knowledge of the symbols and abbreviations used, and this information can be obtained on a special chart—number 5011—issued for this purpose. Also available are charts such as the Stanford series, which includes a coloured lay-out (Admiralty publications are in black and white) and useful inset diagrams that indicate the times of slack water. They are smaller in size than their Admiralty counterparts, being designed for the chart table of the smaller boat.

The next pre-dive check would be on the tide tables, as the dive should coincide with a period of slack water, and this usually (but not always) occurs at the time of maximum high or low tide. High tide usually provides better underwater visibility, especially when diving near the coast.

If possible choose a date on which a neap tide occurs, as neap tides present the least rise and fall in water level, and proportionately less water flow, giving longer usable slack water periods.

Having ascertained the approximate time that you will be diving, examine the chart for tidal stream data. Currents vary greatly in speed at different times of the day, and some points experience dangerous waters even when the area in general is at a slack period.

The telephone provides information on weather conditions in any specific area around Britain, and a call, just before you leave, might save an otherwise wasted journey, for good weather in London does not rule out a force four wind blowing off Dover.

On arrival, obtain from the harbour master information regarding restricted or banned areas, and the fairways used by local boats—these should be avoided.

Also, inform the harbour master where you intend to dive and if you possess, as you should, distress signals, tell him the form they take.

The Tides

It is important, in sea diving, to possess a basic knowledge of tides and their behaviour, for only then can one appreciate the advisability of diving at pre-calculated times. In virtually land-locked areas such as the Mediterranean, tides are no problem to the diver, as the difference between high and low water is only a foot or so: but around Britain, where the tidal range can vary in places from several feet to a gigantic pile-up fifty feet high, it pays to afford tide tables a little attention.

The tides are periodic vertical movements of the seas, brought about by the gravitational pull of the sun and moon. The most powerful influence is that exercised by the moon. This has the effect of drawing water towards the point nearest the moon and creating, in fact, a 'bulge'. The accumulation is duplicated on the opposite side of the world, and when either of these 'bulges' pass a specific area high tide occurs, and it can be seen that there are two perpetual high tides traversing the world. Conversely, either of the flattened 'troughs' that lie between the 'bulges', constitutes a low tide.

As if this were not enough, we then have the gravitational pull of the sun to contend with. The sun, owing to its greater distance from the earth, exerts a gravitational pull only half as powerful as that of the moon. None the less it does wield a magnetic attraction on our waters. When the sun and moon are in line—that is, when the moon is full, or new—the gravitational pull on high tide is intensified and is known as a spring tide (nothing to do with the time of year). When a spring tide occurs the waters will rise higher, and fall lower, than usual. The greater mass of water flooding and ebbing causes tidal streams to flow faster, and for this reason creates difficulties for the diver.

The opposite effect is encountered when the sun and moon are at right angles to each other during the first or third quarter of the moon. Their respective attractions tend to cancel each other out, creating a neap tide. This results in a minimum rise and fall in sea level: the advantages of diving during neap tides have already been mentioned.

Calculating a high tide period is achieved by adding or subtracting a certain length of time from the high tide period of a specific area, known as a tidal constant. For instance, using the times of high water at London Bridge as our tidal constant, we find that high water at Southend is minus one hour and twenty-five minutes from the time quoted for London Bridge, while for Weymouth we would have to add five hours and five minutes. The time of low water will be approximately half-way between two consecutive high water times. Tables of tidal constants, relative to high water at various points around Britain, are published in various nautical almanacs such as Reed's.

When two tidal streams converge—usually just off a point—a condition known as a race occurs. Races are well marked on nautical charts, and can often be seen as a broken, often frothy, patch when the rest of the sea is calm. They are avoided by most vessels and should be similarly treated by divers.

From Shore or Boat

The majority of sea dives are carried out direct from shore, as a boat, although desirable, is not always available—or economical.

When diving from shore, select a spot that has an easy

entry to the water, and several similar points of return. A stretch of coast that has only one point of entry or return might necessitate a long, tiring snorkel back, and in a strong current even this might prove impossible.

The greatest emphasis should be placed on the diver's return to shore. It is not difficult to enter even a comparatively rough sea, but a diver chilled and exhausted, hampered by slippery rocks, surging waves, and laden with equipment, can find the exit a hazardous procedure.

A danger to divers, particularly along breakwaters, is the hook and line of the angler with its threat of laceration and entanglement. Although no sensible diver would enter the water in the vicinity of anglers, the angler might appear on the scene after your submergence. At a time like this your knife is your best friend. If hooked, cut your way out quickly, and don't try to emulate the antics of a very game fish—it does not win that often.

A shore base should be established that is comfortable for those who are not at that moment diving—a lookout who is frozen by biting winds is not capable of carrying out his job efficiently. Ensure that all the equipment is located above the high water mark, and that the lookout or another member of the shore party has a loosely coiled length of rope with a float attached. This can be thrown to any diver who is experiencing difficulty in landing.

A boat gives the diver access to a great number of sites, and for our purposes we can classify them broadly into two types. A dinghy, which is used for short excursions, and its occupants take their seats fully kitted-up, owing to the shortage of space, and secondly, any larger vessel that permits the divers to change on board and, of course, has an almost limitless range.

Considering the cardinal rule 'thou shalt not dive alone', any boat would have a minimum complement of three—two divers plus one lookout–caretaker—although

Plate I. A very edible crab greets the diver at the bottom of Chapman's Pool, Dorset

Photo: L. Zanelli

Plate II. A diver examines the shaft working at the bottom of Stoney Cove, a flooded slate quarry that is a B.S.–A.C., national diving site.

Photo: L. Zanelli

Plate III. Freshwater diving in Llyn Llydaw, North Wales. *Photo* : J. Phoenix

Plate IV. A diver's twinset arises from a visit to the wreck of the *James Egan Layne*.

Photo: L. Zanelli

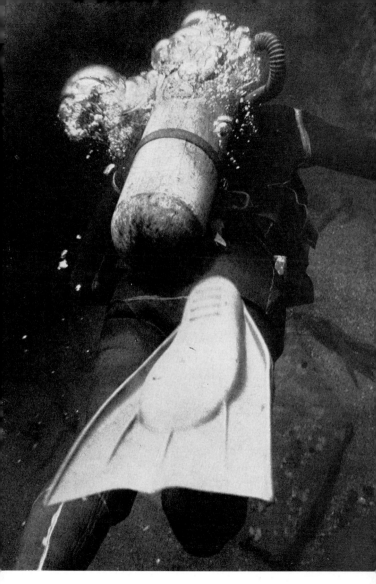

Plate V. Exploring an underwater gully, Dorset.
Photo: L. Zanelli

Plate VI. The cameraman at 45 feet, Stoney Cove.
Photo: L. Zanelli

Plate VII *(top)*. Underwaterscape, Dorset.
Photo : L. Zanelli
(bottom). Diving formation in a Welsh Lake.
Photo : J. Phoenix

Plate VIII (*left*). Pottery from the Roman wreck at Pudding Pan Rock. On display at the British Museum. *Photo :* L. Zanelli (*right*). Mask clearing in a 'dry' suit, and the effects of 'squeeze' can clearly be seen.

Photo : J. Phoenix

this arrangement is only advisable when diving close to shore and in relatively shallow water.

The inflatable dinghy, with an outboard motor (Fig. 7), is an admirable article for short distance work in calm waters. Virtually unsinkable, it lies low in the water, enabling returning divers to ease themselves aboard without much danger of capsizing the vessel. Its compactness when deflated enables it to be carried in the boot of a car and stored in a small space; a useful feature in this motoring age.

On a larger boat much can be done to make diving more enjoyable and safer. The equipment should be stowed, with separate places for wet and dry gear. The same applies to cylinders—a stowage position should be designated for full cylinders, and another, as far away as possible, for empty cylinders. A most useful aquisition should be a sturdy, rigid diving ladder that can be attached to the gunwale, and should be held out from the sides, by angles or framework, to enable a diver with fins on to use it comfortably. Ensure that the bottom rung is well under water and securely tied, for a loose ladder can flail around and injure a diver or damage the boat.

Craft in the vicinity are always a possible danger to divers, so always fly the appropriate flag or flags to warn them off. Unfortunately many week-end sailors are a little weak in their knowledge of flags, so in this case a verbal warning—by loudspeaker—should be used.

Lines should be rigged along the boat, so that divers can hang on while resting, talking, or handing up equipment. If possible, always hand up your heavy gear, weight belt, and aqualung, which will make it easier to climb aboard.

A potential hazard to divers is the screw. Even when in neutral, some screws tend to 'creep', so shut the engine off completely.

Whenever possible, hang a shot line, heavily weighted,

D

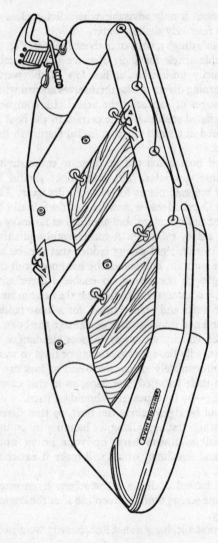

Fig. 7. The Avon 'Redshank', a sturdy example of an inflatable dinghy.

next to the ladder. Divers can then ascend to the point of embarkation, eliminating a snorkel around the boat. Also, in an emergency the anchor, if fouled, may have to be slipped quickly, so ensure that a buoy is fastened outboard on the boat end of the anchor rope.

A long snorkel back to the boat can be an exhausting experience at the end of a dive. If a current is flowing, dive upstream on the outward journey, then you can get a 'free ride' back. Whenever divers have to operate downstream from the boat, secure a float to a long line. The line can then be streamed aft until it is placed over the divers and, on surfacing, the divers can hold the float or line and be hauled in.

Flag Signals

The diver's main use for flag signals is to prevent other vessels from sailing over the area where divers are operating.

There is, unfortunately, no complete international agreement on a flag signifying '*Divers are down, approaching craft keep clear*'. The American Diver's Flag is represented by a white diagonal stripe on a red background, while the British Sub-Aqua Club use—by permission of the Admiralty—the NATO Flag 4, (a white St. Andrew's cross on a red background). This flag signifies 'Divers or friendly underwater demolition personnel down'. Either of these flags should be used in their appropriate waters.

Via the International Code of Signals, a two-letter flag signal can be flown that reads 'I am engaged in submarine survey work—you should keep clear of me. This signal contains the flags H (white and red) and D (blue, with yellow bands top and bottom).

Sometimes divers are tempted to stray from the standard signals just mentioned, and adopt other signals from the International Code, such as K (Stop at once) or T (Do not pass ahead of me), to suit their convenience. Don't do this. It can cause unnecessary confusion.

PART TWO—INLAND

Although inland or fresh water diving cannot hold comparison to a good sea dive, it has many compensations and avenues of interest. The sea is a fickle creature, capable of many moods, and a long journey to the coast can prove disappointing as you stand on the shore watching a force four wind blow up suddenly, ruining the day's diving. Also, many of us live too far from the coast to contemplate regular sea diving. Conditions at inland sites are more predictable, for most lakes, quarries and reservoirs have little or no currents, and the problem of selecting the period of slack water is non-existent.

Stable conditions like these are also ideal for training, as they offer the novice a natural progression from swimming-pool to sea diving. There is also much work that can be carried out in scientific fields. Many lake-beds have never been visited by divers, and are usually rich in legend: there is a 'sunken city', in Lake Bala, a 'monster in Lake Glaslyn', and, of course, Loch Ness—in fact you never know what you might find!

The most popular inland sites are flooded quarries or gravel pits, and lakes. A little diplomacy may be necessary when applying for permission to dive, as angling clubs have snapped up fishing rights to most of the more interesting sites, and tend to take objection to divers.

Lakes

In lakes, underwater visibility is usually adequate, though sometimes a little murky where inlet streams or rivers feed the lake, but away from these sources visibility is normally in the region of 12-15 feet. In Llyn Llydaw, North Wales, vision can exceed 40 feet.

A lake-bed is usually composed of an intriguing blend of rotting leaves, and other vegetation, and mud. The slightest movement will cause this soft sediment to billow up in dense clouds, reducing vision to inches for a considerable time, so if another diving party is following you, or you think you might have to double back, or across, your path at some point, it is best to swim several feet above the bottom of the lake, and 'touch down' only when you sight something of interest.

Lakes often have surprising depth. In areas of rock, or limestone, vegetable and animal life is often sparse, and the clearness of the water enables light to penetrate down to the bottom, but in areas of a softer land formation, prolific flora and fauna cause particles of matter to be released into the water and, along with other suspended sediment, filter the light on its downward journey. If the depth is considerable complete darkness will envelope the bottom. In these conditions torches are a must, and divers should be roped, either together, in pairs (with a wrist-to wrist 'buddy' line), or singly, on a line to a surface tender, for in lake diving the danger of swimming into the branches of a submerged tree is very real.

On lakes used for boating, always dive in conjunction with a surface dinghy following your bubbles. Divers ascending quickly can arrive in collision with a moving vessel, and if the vessel is motorised, the surface could become strewn with shredded neoprene and divers' pieces! Show the diving flag on the dinghy and verbally warn approaching craft away. In any case, lakes are often a deceptive distance in diameter, and even if the waters are not used for boating it is wise, with inexperienced divers in the party, to use a dinghy. A float (a car inner tube will do), directed by a surface snorkel cover,

that a tired diver could utilise to take a breather, is also
excellent.

On a more cheerful note, there is always the chance of
stumbling upon a 'wreck'. This might be only an old
rowing boat in the last stages of decay, but could be some
larger and more recent submergence, in which case you
can proceed with salvage negotiations.

Reservoirs

Reservoirs often present useful diving grounds—sizeable
surface areas of water and sometimes good depth. The
constant turnover of water usually means a denser amount
of suspended sediment—and proportionately reduced
visibility—but in the case of very large reservoirs, they
can be treated much the same as a lake—indeed many
are in fact converted from natural lakes.

Swimming of any kind is banned in direct drinking
reservoirs, but sometimes allowed in other types, so
ensure that permission is obtained before diving takes
place. Also check with the engineer regarding the position
and flow of the outlet valves and any other potential
hazards.

Canals

The canal is usually prolific in aquatic life, but the
presence of luxurious plant growth and fish life is of very
little interest to the diver when vision is reduced to a
couple of inches, and this is often the case. Canals are
universally regarded as a rubbish dump, thus the possibility of encountering rusting bedsteads and bicycle-
frames—allied with zero visibility—can constitute a
danger to the most experienced diver. When visibility is
bad it is usually better to cancel a dive, and this applies
particularly to canals. 'Retired' canals sometimes offer

clear water and an interesting dive, especially if the diver
has an interest in, and knowledge of, biology—or junk.
The shallow depth enables a considerable amount of
time to be spent under water, and a lot of research could
be carried out on these man-made waterways.

Quarries and Gravel Pits

Flooded quarries and gravel pits are popular training
sites for diving clubs. Access to the water is usually
convenient, and if the 'diving rights' are purchased, the
owner will sometimes allow changing facilities to be
installed.

If the quarry or pit is still being worked, visibility will
probably be hopeless, but if disused, reasonable conditions can exist. Like canals, these sites are favoured for
rubbish disposal and can contain even larger items of
danger, such as old cars.

Rivers

Rivers that contain strong currents and poor visibility
rank among the most dangerous of diving locations—the
Thames is a good example—along with swift-moving
mountain waters, and these are dealt with in a section for
more advanced diving. None the less, rivers in non-
industrial, rocky areas sometimes contain deep clear
pockets or pools—below a waterfall for instance or on the
outside of an acute bend—and can provide good year-
round diving.

Having ploughed through the section on physics, you
will know that fresh water has a buoyancy index different
to that of salt water; in practical use this means that a
weight belt balanced for a sea dive will need 2–3 pounds
of lead removed before a fresh water excursion.

Although inland waters abound with a great variety of

edible fish, the diving gourmet will have to be content
with mere observation of succulent trout, salmon, etc.,
or at most a photograph, for the Salmon and Freshwater
Fisheries Act of 1923 renders it illegal to use 'A spear or
like instrument for the purpose of taking salmon, trout
or fresh water fish'; and just you try catching them with
your bare hands!

VIII. Rescue and Life Saving

Accidents and difficult situations can befall even the best-planned diving excursion, for water is an alien medium for man to work in. On the surface, the aqualung diver, encumbered as he is by weighty equipment, is very vulnerable—probably more so than any other kind of swimmer.

The method of rescue and type of treatment afforded the distressed diver depends upon a quick assessment of the circumstances by the rescuer. Condition of the subject, distance and time required for getting him back to shore or boat, ease with which he can be towed, ease of landing the subject—all have to be taken into account in the briefest possible time: a few seconds delay—in calculating or carrying out the action—can mean all the difference between life and death.

The Royal Life Saving Society does magnificent work in furthering the teaching of life saving. Anyone connected with a water-sport would do well to study their handbook, and attempt to obtain one of the awards granted by the Society.

In addition to standard rescue and treatment methods, the underwater swimmer requires further techniques—particularly in the field of rescue—that are applicable to the modern frogman.

Methods of Rescue

Should a diver lose consciousness under water, his life will depend upon his companion being able to carry out quick, efficient rescue drill. The rescuer should grasp the subject firmly by an arm, just above the elbow, removing first the subject's weight belt, and then his own. If this procedure is reversed, there is a danger of the rescuer floating immediately upwards. During the ascent, which should be smooth and steady, ensure that the casualty is breathing out—or that the expanding air in his lungs is escaping. Should there be no sign of air issuing from the lips or demand valve, press his stomach and ensure that it does.

Whether or not to inflate a life-jacket while under water depends upon the circumstances: if the rescuer is in full control of the unconscious diver, then it is probably better to wait until the surface is reached. On surfacing, at least the victim's life-jacket should be inflated, using the automatic mechanism; unless he can be landed *immediately*, mouth-to-mouth resuscitation should be attempted on the spot if he is no longer breathing.

A swimmer who is on the surface and in distress is a different proposition. Even a person of small dimensions can be a dangerous handful when struggling and panic-stricken. Caution is needed at all times: the victim might seem quite calm as you approach, only to burst into frenzied activity when the rescuer reaches grasping distance.

When swimming out to attempt a rescue, it is important to keep your head out of the water with your eyes trained on the victim. If your gaze should be diverted—even for a second—it is odds on that he will disappear under water at that precise moment. Also, never approach a distressed swimmer from the front: do so carefully from behind, and grasp him securely by the arms, just above the elbows, holding him in this position until he has calmed down and is ready for a tow.

The method of towing depends upon the condition of the person being towed. If he is calm, and if he is wearing an inflated life-jacket, he could lay on his back and place his hands upon the rescuer's shoulders, who could then fin forward in the usual manner. Should the victim have no life-jacket, however, this method could prove hazardous in the event of a sudden panic. In this circumstance, the rescuer should grasp the victim by the upper arms while propelling him home. The important point is never to get into a position where the victim can grasp you fully.

Artificial Respiration

Hundreds of years ago, there was a strange method of artificial respiration in vogue. It consisted of blowing air into the lungs, via a nostril, with a pair of bellows. The ensuing years saw many 'superior' systems evolve. In Laborde's method, the victim's tongue was seized between the folds of a handkerchief, jerked forward, and then allowed to return to the mouth; this action was repeated 15–20 times a minute. The Silvester method required manipulation of the victim's arms while he was stretched on his back. A Shafer method graduate, on the other hand, placed the victim face down, and kept up a steady pressure on the back at the lower ribs.

Currently, the expired air method—referred to in the popular Press as 'the kiss of life'—is considered the most efficient. The procedure here is for the rescuer to place his mouth over the victim's, while pinching shut the latter's nostrils, and to blow air into his lungs. It can be seen that the expired air method is, in principle, identical to the first method mentioned—except that the ancients introduced an element of sophistication with the bellows. It has taken mankind a couple of centuries to appreciate the efficiency of this aged system.

The expired air method is of particular importance to the free-diver. When a person has ceased breathing, it is

essential that artificial respiration be carried out without
delay: a long tow back to land or boat could prove fatal.
The expired air method is the only system that can permit artificial respiration to be carried out while victim and
rescuer are still in the water.

The normal technique for carrying out expired air
resuscitation is as follows: place the victim on his back so
that his chest is raised slightly higher than his stomach;
ensure that his mouth is clear of obstruction, and tilt his
head well back; place your mouth over the victim's, seal
his nostrils by pinching them with your fingers, and
blow. After exhaling, turn your head to see that his chest
is falling (if it is not, check that the mouth and throat are
clear of obstruction, and try again). When starting, give a
half-dozen quick inflations, reducing gradually to fifteen
per minute.

Small children and babies require a slightly modified
expired air technique. The rescuer can probably cover
the baby's mouth and nose at the same time, avoiding
having to pinch its nostrils. Respiration is carried out at
the rate of 20 *gentle* puffs per minute. Never blow vio-
lently into a baby's lungs.

The expired air system will introduce life-giving
oxygen into the lungs at a better rate than any manual
system, and is the method of artificial respiration preferred by the Royal Life Saving Society.

In training, never practise mouth-to-mouth resuscitation on another person by actually going through the
procedure of blowing into his or her lungs. The risk of
spreading infection will more than offset the benefit of the
technique gained.

External Heart Massage

If, in addition to the cessation of respiration, the heart
has ceased to function, then external heart massage should

be given as soon as possible. This is ideally carried out by two operators, one applying expired air artificial respiration, and the other external heart massage. Should there be only one operator—as is often the case—then one inflation of the victim's lungs by the expired air method should be followed by ten external heart compressions, as follows.

Lay the victim on a firm flat surface, face up. Place the heel of the palm of one hand, with your other hand on top of it, over the lower half of the breastbone (sternum). Rock forward, using your weight to exert a pressure that will depress the breastbone at least an inch. Rock backward, decreasing the pressure. Repeat at a rate of 60 compressions per minute, though slightly faster, and with much less pressure, for children. In the case of a baby, only two fingers, applying sharp but gentle pressure, are required.

As with expired air resuscitation, external heart massage should never actually be practised on another person in training. A couple of broken ribs—of little consequence to the casualty whose heart has stopped beating—can cause some annoyance to the person being used as a dummy!

IX. Diving Sites, Services, and Facilities

There is, unfortunately, very little literature available on diving sites, services and facilities. The free-diver seeking different waters usually has to rely on trial-and-error principles, while the location of the nearest compressor might be found—with luck—in the classified columns of one of the many diving magazines, provided the compressor owners advertise and you subscribe to all the magazines!

This chapter, then, is an attempt to give a rough sketch of the United Kingdom from the underwater swimmer's point of view. A really comprehensive survey would fill at least one large volume—thus in this limited space only the surface can be scratched. The information contained here should prove valuable to the free-diver who travels outside his local area. It has been compiled, mostly, from information supplied by the secretaries of many British Sub-Aqua Club branches, whose generous and unselfish participation deserves recognition from all underwater swimmers. Part has been compiled by the writer, from personal experience, and the remainder supplied by various commercial enterprises.

The chapter has been sectioned into specific areas: South, from Dover westwards, to Land's End, including the Channel Islands; West, from Land's End northwards to the Scottish Border, including Wales and the Isle of Man; Scotland; East, from the east Scottish Border southwards to Dover, including London; Ireland, north and south; and Holidays Abroad.

The British Oxygen Company can supply medically pure air at many depots throughout the United Kingdom. But this facility is only a minute part of the B.O.C.'s activities, and in some cases a wait of a day or two might prove necessary. The best procedure is to write or telephone in advance, and obtain relevant details. Of course, this also applies to any other source of air or services; always inquire in advance for any change in services or facilities. For the sake of convenience a list of B.O.C. depots that will supply air is given at the end of this book.

PART ONE—THE SOUTH

From Dover to Land's End; and the Channel Islands

At the time of writing there is no regular supply of compressed air in the Dover area—at least, there is not one known to the writer. The harbour can provide reasonable diving, but the permission of the harbour master must be obtained. At nearby Fans Bay, lie the few remains of the *Preussen*. A five-masted full-rigged vessel of 5081 tons, she ground ashore on November 6th, 1910 after a collision, and parts are still visible at low tide.

Farther along, at Pevensey Bay, lies the 60-gun *Resolution*, sunk in 1703.

Almost due south of Eastbourne, the 6,610 ton *Oceana* sank on March 16th, 1912. She carried a cargo of gold bars, silver, and coin to the value of nearly £800,000. Most of this was recovered, but a quantity still lies at the bottom.

The main problem in this general area is the poor visibility near shore. However, if you can get out in a boat, some excellent diving can be obtained. In this respect the Brighton area has much to offer. The Brighton and Worthing branch of the B.S-A.C. can supply air at their headquarters: Lighthouse Club, Brighton Road, Shoreham-by-Sea. The branch also has its own boat, the *Blue Dolphin*. This vessel is available for charter on most week-ends and can accommodate up to twenty divers. The *Blue Dolphin* skipper will take you to any of the local sites. These include the Outer Jenny Rocks, beside which there is a wreck of unknown name. The Rocks support good quantities of flat fish, bass, and conger. Near Hove Lagoon, Roman remains have been found, catering for the archaeologist.

At nearby Newhaven, local boats are easy to charter. Good diving can be obtained along the seaward side of the west breakwater (beware the anglers' lines and hooks), and crab and lobster inhabit the jumbled concrete base. Four miles off Newhaven, the wreck of the trawler *Celtic*, sunk in 1947, is also a favourite with anglers. The wreck of a German submarine is reputed to be in the vicinity, but it has never been found.

At Shoreham, underwater equipment can be obtained from Shoreham Watersports, The Old Watch House, Shoreham-by-Sea (Telephone: Southwick 3469). About a mile off Shoreham is the wreck of the *Miown*, sunk in 1911. Farther out are supposedly several wrecks, the result of war, but none have been found to date.

Just off Worthing, due south, lies the wreck of the *Indiana*, reposing on the bottom since 1901.

Farther west, Hayling Island juts into the sea. Much of the southern portion of the Island now lies under the sea, and investigations are being made into material found at the sea-bed which might prove to be the foundations of a building.

The area south of Portsmouth contains many wrecks: the 60-gun *Mary Rose* (1545); the *Royal George* (1782); and the *Newcastle* (1703)—to name a few. An active search is currently being undertaken for the first named. At nearby Southampton, cylinder charging facilities can be obtained through the sports store of Oswald Bailey Ltd., 109 Above Bar.

The Needles, at the north-west point of the Isle of Wight, have been the cause of many wrecks. The best known is probably the 40-gun warship *Insurance*. Wrecked in 1753, she was carrying the Governor of Jamaica home, and many valuables are reputed to have been on board. It requires little knowledge of mathematics to work out this equation: many wrecks = dangerous waters, and the Needles are no exception. Only experienced divers with local knowledge should attempt to dive in the area.

There are two associated sports stores nearby that can supply equipment and cylinder-charging facilities: Oswald Bailey, 34 Commercial Road, Bournemouth; and Calypso Sports, 16–18 Bournemouth Road, Parkstone, Poole. The latter lays claim to being the largest watersports store in Europe.

The Solent is a rather shallow channel, and visibility tends to deteriorate rapidly. Tides also can be rather fierce, so dive only at neap tide or slack water. Spearfishermen find the Solent, when conditions are right, an excellent area for flatfish, bass, and mullet, etc.

The Poole–Bournemouth area, although rich in flatfish, is usually too cloudy for underwater activities, except way off-shore, although patient spear-fishermen can be well rewarded.

Swanage is rapidly becoming the sub-aquatic centre for the south of England, and this is due in no small measure to the facilities provided by Bob and Dennis Wright, who run a diving school on the pier. The

Wrights can supply air, boat, equipment, tuition and accommodation. For bookings phone Swanage 3565. The School of Archaeology runs its courses from here. Swanage Bay is an excellent site for underwater swimmers of all grades. An anchor-studded reef runs along the bay, and life in the form of mullet, flatfish, bass and crabs can usually be found. The area is deficient in diveable wrecks. Those available are located in deep, dangerous waters.

Round the corner from Swanage, Tilly Wim provides a popular site, although by virtue of its location, care must be taken with the nippy tides. Tilly Wim is the starting-point for the vast seaweed jungles that stretch along the English Channel as far as Land's End. The huge fronds afford accommodation to a great variety of marine life, and a diver can virtually climb hand-over-hand along the weed's tough stalks against a sturdy current.

Durdle Door and the adjacent Man O' War Cove offer excellent diving in sheltered conditions, but the walk down—and more so the climb back—calls for a tough constitution. It is wiser to hire a boat from nearby Lulworth Cove, itself a useful site when conditions are right.

Weymouth Bay is noted for bass and crab, and usually provides good diving. Ron Parry, at 43 Walpole Street, Weymouth (Telephone: Weymouth 1712), can provide air, accommodation, and a five-berth, 36-ft. boat complete with echo-sounder. Ron can pinpoint all the local wrecks, such as the *Himalaya*, and is currently searching for the *Earl of Abergavenny*, an East India boat which sank somewhere out in the bay in 1805. The captain was Wordsworth, brother of the famous poet, and the vessel is said to have contained gold. Ron has found lamps, flints and muskets, and needless to say is hoping that the gold will come next.

Portland Bill is the haunt of large crab and conger. Extreme care must, however, be taken regarding tides, for the notorious Portland Race lies at the end of the Bill, and this turbulent stretch of water is dangerous for even sturdy boats, let alone a swimmer.

The sweep of Chesil Bank provides good crab-hunting grounds, but care should be taken of the steady current.

Lyme Bay can provide good diving from several points. Boats can be chartered from Lyme Regis, Seaton and Sidmouth. Out in the Bay lie many wrecks worth a visit. One and a half miles south-west of Lyme Regis is the location of the 3,000-ton *Baygitano*, sunk in 1918 in seventy feet of water. Farther west, off Dawlish, lies the 6,000-ton *Gallicia*, sunk by a mine in 1917, in fifty feet of water. Most of the Lyme Bay wrecks display gorgonia coral growing on the remains, and are inhabited by pout and pollack in addition to the usual crab and conger.

Curving S.W. into Torquay, we are in the home waters of the Torbay Branch B.S-A.C., and some very good diving areas. Torbay Branch meet every Monday evening at the Royal Torbay Yacht Club, Beacon Hill, Torquay. Throughout the summer, and at other times by arrangement, air is available at their air filling station: No. 10 Store, Beacon Quay, Torquay Harbour. The Branch can put you in touch with boat owners available for charter; they publish a unique and valuable booklet, 'Diving Sites in South Devon', priced at a mere 1s. 6d. plus S.A.E.

A good flatfish site in the vicinity is Anstey's Cove. A car park is situated at the top, and it is a short descent to the beach. The bottom is sandy with rocky outcrops, and the depth, depending on the tide, twenty to thirty feet.

At Brixham a good dive can be obtained from the breakwater, in the outer harbour, or the beach on the seaward side. Dive in the outer harbour if conditions are rough at sea, but watch out for heavy water traffic—scallops, crab, mullet and starfish can be found around the soft bottom, and conger along the rugged breakwater base. Beware, too, of anglers' lines. When conditions are good, the beach makes a good dive: dense marine vegetation commences almost immediately, and large crabs have been found.

Dartmouth is the location of Capt. T. A. Hampton's British Underwater Centre, at the Boat Cottage, Warfleet Creek (Telephone: Dartmouth 298). The B.U.C. can supply compressed air, by arrangement. Diving in the Dart estuary itself, without experienced company, should be avoided. As with most estuaries, strong currents and poor visibility occur, particularly on the ebb tide. Divers wishing to cruise the area—the only way to reach many of the best sites—are well catered for. F. R. Dayes, Bottom Flat, 73 Above Town, Dartmouth, can supply an 86-ton converted Brixham sailing trawler, the *Boy Eric*. The boat has a very civilized amenity not usually available on this type of vessel—a saloon (with bar).

Farther along the coast, South Devon Divers, Farewell House, Stoke Fleming (Telephone Stoke Fleming 271), will provide the 12-ton trawler *Lady Mildred*. *Mildred* can take a dozen divers, and has a compressor installed aboard, so if you find that sunken treasure you can dive all day!

Salcombe usually provides good clear water—even in the estuary—although the water traffic is heavy. Air can be obtained from the Salcombe Motor and Marine Co., Central Garage, and a boat from Mike Dornom, 2 Croft View, Island Street. Lying inside Blackstone Rock, Salcombe Estuary, on an even keel, is the wreck of the 136-ton *Placidas Farroult*. Sunk in 1940, the wreck is still in good condition and, at the time of writing, safe for an experienced diver to enter. There is just one cabin, with an electric cooker in the corner! The last sheltered cove between Salcombe and the open sea is Starhole Bay, an excellent beginners' site that is also the location of

the wreck of the four-masted barque *Herzogin Cecilie*.
Little remains of this proud vessel, run aground in 1936;
she would complete the Australia–England run with
5,000 tons of grain in her holds.

Newton Ferrers is the home of scallop, mullet, conger,
and monk fish. Boats are available for hire. At the mouth
of Ferrers is Gt. Mewstone, an island-rock approachable
only by boat, but offering a well-gullied weed-covered
bottom inhabited by pollack, bass, crab, and sea urchins.
If you really feel adventurous, and the sea is calm, get a
good boat to take you eleven miles out to the Eddystone
Lighthouse. Eddystone provides visibility that one can
never obtain near shore—nearly 100 feet has been recorded—really large wrasse, pollack and bass abound, in
addition to crab, lobster and sea urchins. Other offshore
locations in the vicinity are the Rutts-East and West—
and Hands Deep.

West of Plymouth, in Whitsand Bay, lies what is
without doubt the most dived-on wreck in British Waters.
The 7,000-ton *James Egan Layne*, a Liberty ship, was
built in 1944 and torpedoed the same year. Upright, on
an even keel, the wreck lies in eighty feet of water, and a
swim along the promenade deck, resplendent with
gorgonia coral, and passing pollack, is a memorable
experience.

Looe has been the centre for many spear-fishing con-
tests, evidence of the prolific fish life in this area. Con-
tinuing our journey westward, nearly every cove and bay
encountered can, when conditions are right, offer good
diving.

In Penzance, air is available from no less than three
compressors, all operated by 'Watersports', Albert Street
(Telephone: Penzance 4157). 'Watersports' also have a
portable compressor for hire, for use on remote sites.
The area around Penzance contains hundreds of wrecks.
To name but a few, there are the minesweeper *Royallo*,

the coaster *Primrose*, and a 10,000-ton cargo ship, the
Heliopes, all in one hundred feet of water in Mounts Bay,
a mere ten-minute boat trip. Near Lamorna, the *Juan
Ferrar* is an almost 'new' (1964) wreck. A tanker, *St.
Gwenole* went down near Penberth, with the distant-
water trawler *Verts Praires* nearby. On the Runnel Stone
there is the *City of Westminster*, and many others unidenti-
fied. Another recent wreck, off Land's End, is the distant-
water trawler *Jean Gougi*. At Newquay Bay there are six
known wrecks in less than 100 feet of water. Information
regarding boat charter and the location of these, and
many other wrecks, can be obtained from 'Watersports'.

Should your inclination be towards luxury cruising,
then contact Dave Ellison, 60 Farnham Road, Guildford,
Surrey. Dave is the agent for what is claimed to be the
only luxury vessel in full-time charter commission for
skin diving and deep sea fishing holidays in the U.K.
A 65-ft. motor yacht, with air, diving equipment, T.V.
and bar, the vessel is available for cruising the warm Gulf
Stream waters of Devon, Cornwall and the Channel
Islands.

The Channel Islands are unique in the U.K. Nowhere
else can you get such a variation and choice of totally
different underwater scenery by merely driving to
another bay, which is never more than a few minutes
away. The warm clear waters of the Gulf Stream are the
reason for the excellent diving, but these same waters can
exert fierce currents when the tide is ripe, and it is
always safest to dive with an experienced local diver.

Around Jersey, apart from an abundance of wrecks, the
underwater swimmer can expect to find lobster, mullet,
pollack, bass and skate. The Jersey Underwater Centre,
Water's Edge Hotel, Bouley Bay can supply air, a full
range of equipment (including underwater cameras and
spear guns), and owns a 36-ft. diving boat.

Guernsey divers are catered for by the Guernsey

Diving Club, at Del Mar Court, Le Varclin, St. Martin's. The Club can provide accommodation, air, and a full range of equipment, and has compiled a chart of no less than three hundred wrecks, including the recent (1965) 4,500-ton *La Sale*. Guernsey underwater life includes crayfish, lobster, red and grey mullet, bass, garfish, pollack, and ormers. The last named is a local shell fish found only in Guernsey waters.

Nearby Herm and Sark also offer excellent diving, but a boat will have to be chartered from Jersey or Guernsey —preferably from one of the organisations named, as local diving knowledge is essential in these variable waters.

PART TWO—THE WEST

From Land's End to Wales; the Lake District; and the Isle of Man

The coast of North Cornwall has a succession of bays and coves suitable for diving, but tidal currents are usually stronger and more unpredictable than those on the south side. It would be unthinkable to arrive in the Land's End area without a dive at, or near, the End itself. Access to Land's End is via the A.30 road. Currents, however, make the dive hazardous—it is better to try the adjacent Sennen Cove, where car-parking facilities are available. Just off shore, at the western side of the bay, an assortment of rocks called the Tribbens jut out of 20 feet of water, providing an interesting dive. At nearby Whitesand Bay, in 35 feet of water, lies the remains of the S.S. *Beau Maris*, sunk in 1914. Tidal currents can be strong. Farther along, off the B.3300 road, Porthreath lies in a bay. A car park is available, and good diving can be obtained off the beach. Almost a half-mile off shore two rocks—Horse and Gull—rise out of 60 feet of water, providing accommodation for pollack, wrasse, conger and crab. The nearest source of air known to the writer along this area is from R. D. Booker, 19 Slade Valley Road, Ilfracombe, Devon, on any evening from 6 p.m. until 7 p.m. Diving around Ilfracombe is very good, but obtain information locally regarding the strong currents. This also applies to the whole Bristol Channel area. The sports store of Oswald Bailey, 61 Horsefair, Bristol 1, can obtain air from the facilities nearby.

The South Wales coast, according to local divers, is generally restricted owing to poor visibility, although Oxwich Bay, Gower, is useful around July-August. There is a wreck in the bay, visible at low water, with a nasty current passing just off the seaward side. Along the Pembrokeshire coast, the local information on sites refers to Martin's Haven, Broad Haven, St. David's, and Sheep's Island. For the latter, a boat will have to be chartered from nearby Milford Haven. The Newport and Cardiff Branch B.S-A.C. have a compressor situated in Cardiff, and anyone wishing to avail themselves of this facility should contact the Equipment Officer, Mr. Arthur Vick, 71 Eye Street, Splott, Cardiff. Air is also obtainable from the British Oxygen Co., and Air Products, both in Cardiff.

Little information is available regarding the centre of the Welsh coast, but a submerged forest lies off Borth, and Aberdovey offers reasonable diving around the harbour, but the permission of the Master must be obtained.

Tremadoc Bay is fairly shallow, with a sandy bottom, and not really suitable for diving. It has, however, the interest of being the location where the *Santa Cruz*, carrying £500,000 in gold, was lost in 1820. At nearby

Abersoch, a boat may be chartered to Porth Caered, where really good diving can be obtained—as it can around the whole Lleyn promontory. Air can be obtained, with prior notice, from Butterworth's Garage, Morfa Nefyn (Telephone: Nefyn 210). Boats are available for charter from Morfa Nefyn, with a local skipper who knows the area well. Contact H. Williams, 158 Oulton Road, Stone, Staffs.

The island of Anglesey is invaded most week-ends by a battery of underwater swimmers, and with good reason. Clear water, wrecks, and marine life abound, and one can always cross the island to the side sheltered from the wind. Near Moelfre is the wrecking point of the *Royal Charter*, documented by Alexander McKee in his book *The Golden Wreck*. Wrecks nearby are the M.V. *Hindlea*, the S.S. *Missouri*, at Porth da Fach, the S.S. *Primrose Hill*, off North Stack, and the S.S. *Cambank*, six miles off Moelfre. Ravens Point and Porth da Garon (Waterlily Cove) are probably the most dived-on sites on the Welsh coastline. Other popular spots are Cemaes Bay, Church Bay, Bull Bay, Porth Eilian, and Point Lynas. When conditions at sea are too rough, there are plenty of clear water quarries, and a short car ride will take you to the lakes of Snowdonia. Diving services and facilities are more than adequate in Anglesey, due to the presence of J. Leyland-Smart, Traeth Bychan House, Marianglas, Moelfre (Telephone: Cressington Park 3027). Leyland-Smart can provide air, accommodation (house, caravan, or camping), boats, with or without an attendant guide, and equipment.

The North-West is pictorially famous for its Lake District. These inland stretches of water provide the underwater swimmer with a large area of water that is unaffected by tide or weather. Lakes do not possess the variety of underwater scenery that is available at sea, but conditions are more reliable, and there are many

good-sized wrecks lying at the bottom of some of the
larger lakes. The Isle of Man is bidding, with every prospect of success, to become the U.K. Diving Centre. The
advantage of diving from an island is that there is
invariably a sheltered bay or beach available within a
short drive. Around the Isle of Man, currents are not so
fierce as those in the Channel Islands, and the water can
be just as clear—although colder. When the wind is
easterly, suggested sites are: Port Erin, Fleshwick Bay,
Niarbyl, Glen Maye, and Peel, which are all on the west
coast. When the wind is westerly, Langness Point, and
Cornaa, on the East coast, are suggested, but a powerful
current runs off the former. Air is available from the
Marine Biological Station, at Port Erin—apply between
9 a.m. and 4.30 p.m., Monday to Friday—and from the
Fire Service, Murray House, Douglas, during the same
periods. The Isle of Man Sub-Aqua Club provides a hire
service for lead weights. This can be of invaluable help
to divers transporting gear by plane. Contact the
Secretary, E. H. Maley, 'Mount Vernon', Belmont Hill,
Douglas.

PART THREE—SCOTLAND

Although the Scots are renowned as warm-hearted
hosts, they are invariably pessimistic about their own
beautiful country. The usual reply to a question on
diving is to the effect that they welcome visitors, and hope
that many divers come to Scotland—'Despite our bad
weather and cold water'. This last remark contains the
canny Scot's defence against the holiday diver. It is
meant to deter all but those interested in diving for
diving's sake—and quite rightly, for Scotland possesses

some of the finest diving waters in the world. It was Lieutenant George Wookey, M.B.E., R.N., who first let the cat out of the bag when he stated that in his opinion Scotland possessed the world's finest diving—and this just after he had returned from New Zealand. And if you have not heard of Lieutenant Wookey it is time you brushed up on your diving history, for as far back as 1956 he broke the world diving record by diving to 600 feet and remaining there for five minutes.

Commencing from the south-west, the first site to report is a promontory jutting out West of Stranraer. Honeycombed with bays, the choice site is at the south end, the Mull of Galloway. At this point, vertical cliffs plunge abruptly into 150 feet or more of clear water, with fish in abundance.

Farther north, the Firth of Clyde is noted for large lobster, and at Millport, on the nearby Great Cumbrae Island, is the Scottish Marine Biological Station that will welcome visitors. The island itself is a good diving area: Millport is situated at a bay with 30 feet of water, Keppel Pier abounds in marine life, and you can shelve off into 80 feet of water. The isle of Arran is a popular holiday location that provides excellent diving. It is served by steamer from Ardrossan, daily except Sunday. At Lamlash Bay, car access is available to a shingle beach, where the maximum depth is 120 feet, with plenty of flatfish in the shallows, and the vista faces unexplored Holy Island. Horse Isle, just off Ardrossan, needs to be a boat dive. Permission must be obtained as it is a bird sanctuary. But the diving is extremely interesting, with plenty of marine life at depths up to 50 feet. Off Porten-cross is the site of a reputed Spanish galleon wreck. In about 1790, a diver brought up some cannons, but searches since have proved fruitless. Around the Cloch Lighthouse is an 80 feet channel of dark water, at the bottom of which reside queen scallops and large whelks.

After Cloch Point, the Firth becomes industrial, the river extending to Glasgow in a series of sand and mud flats.

This corner of Scotland is well endowed with air facilities. The G.M.T. Diving Company, 520 St. Vincent Street, Glasgow, C.3 (Telephone: CIT 3916), can provide all sub-aqua requirements. The Clydebank Branch of the Scottish Sub-Aqua Club have a compressor located at the home of Mr. J. MacBeath, 4 Brook Street, Dalmuit. Bottles are usually filled on Thursday evenings, but in any case write first.

Scotland is famous for its lochs, and the variety that have one end open to the sea are of great interest to the underwater swimmer, containing salt and fresh water in varying proportions. Loch Long is a good example. The sides of the loch slope quickly down to 50 feet, and here are found lobster and conger. Nearby Gare Loch and Loch Goil are similar, but local divers insist that the finest diving in the area is available at Loch Fyne. It was after diving here that Lieutenant Wookey is reputed to have made his statement.

Diving and facilities in the Oban area are superb, due mainly to the presence of the Oban Branch S.S-A.C. The Branch has an excellent hut situated near the water's edge at Dungallan Pards on the south side of the bay. A compressor is installed, and air can be provided for visiting clubs and private divers. The relatively small size of the fish does not make spear-fishing popular—and this applies to Scotland in general—but Oban provides abundant marine life, clear water, and a wreck 'on the doorstep', in the middle of the bay in 60 feet of water. Shellfish are really prolific, lobster, crab, and queen scallop. The very helpful A. McLennan, Secretary of the Branch, can be located at Park Gate Cottages, Duncraggan Road, Oban.

Farther north-west, the Hebrides contain a great

number of wrecks, the most famous of which was the subject of Compton Mackenzie's *Whisky Galore*. Yes, the story *was* based on fact. Indeed Royal Navy divers recently found the wreck, and salvaged many bottles of whisky, led by none other than Lieutenant Wookey. Perhaps here we have the key to his affection for Scottish water!

Enough has been written about Loch Ness and its famous monster without elaboration here. Suffice to say that the Loch is over 600 feet deep, cold, and has strong currents.

Ullapool is the northern equivalent of Polperro—some say better. Within a stone's throw off shore lies a wreck in 60 feet of water. There is no air supply known at the time of writing, but if you possess several cylinders the trip is well worth while.

The islands north of Scotland are virgin diving territory. Scapa Flow, in the Orkneys, has reputedly incredible visibility (the reverse 'incredible visibility' to that of the Thames) and, of course the scuttled German fleet. The Shetlands have the unlocated site of the Dutch treasure ship *Camerlands*, sunk somewhere on the Outer Skerries, and in Gulberwick Bay lie the remains of the Viking ships *Fifa* and *Hjalp*. Although sunk in 1151, and possibly impossible to trace, there was an appreciable amount of gold aboard, and gold does not perish in sea water.

The east coast of Scotland is not as indented as the west, but the tidal currents are not, on average, as fierce. Just north of Aberdeen lie the remains of an Armada galleon. Divers have never pin-pointed the remains, but in the last century, fishing trawls hauled up cannons. These guns were placed on the ramparts of Balmoral Castle.

For a short way south of Aberdeen, visibility is poor. Off Dundee, the handicap of poor visibility is countered by the great interest of a small area where, in 1651, over fifty vessels sank in a violent storm. The plunder that went down in these ships is reported to be worth nearly £3,000,000.

Within sight of the Mecca of golf—St. Andrews—water once more becomes clear and most diveable, south from St. Andrews Bay. At Edinburgh, Lillywhites of 129, Princess Street can supply equipment, while air can be obtained, by appointment, from the Edinburgh Branch B.S-A.C. Contact the Secretary, Lt.-Col. A. Gordon-Rogers (Retd.), O.B.E., T.D., at 49, Ainbry Court, St. Nicholas-at-Falcon Gardens, Edinburgh 10.

North Berwick is a popular site. Boats can be chartered, and a trip to Bass Rock, a bird sanctuary, is worth while. A wreck lies somewhere close, and sea urchins and lobster can be located down to 100 feet. Dunbar, nearby, is also a popular site where diving is usually carried out from the Harbour.

St. Abbs has such a good reputation that it is invaded most week-ends by fervents from England's North-East. Boats can be chartered, and the skippers know all the good spots. Air is available, by arrangement, from the Eyemouth and District Sub-Aqua Club, by contacting Mrs. Robin Collin, Craigeilan, High Street, Eyemouth (Telephone: 305). Eyemouth itself was the setting of a great tragedy, when a gale destroyed much of its fishing fleet in 1881 with considerable loss of life.

PART FOUR—THE EAST

From the North-East to Dover; and London

The east coast of England is the poorest section of our round trip, owing to the softer coastal structure, and the sands of the Dogger Bank in the North Sea. However, there are sites where good diving can be obtained, especially if you charter a boat to take you out a little way. Acomb House, Hexham, Northumberland, is the home of Submarine Products, who produce a variety of underwater equipment. But being manufacturers, they provide no facilities, and air is obtained from the British Oxygen Co. in this area.

Just off Redcar, Whitby, and Scarborough, are many wrecks attainable by chartering a boat. Cleveland Diving and Marine Products, Prospect Terrace, Marske-by-the-Sea, Redcar (Telephone: Redcar 4322), can arrange supplies of compressed air, and are suppliers of equipment, suits, etc. Mr. Maughan, the Managing Director, is a keen diver who can give you all the information on the area you need. Air can also be obtained, by arrangement, from Scarborough Branch B.S-A.C., at 25, St. Mary's Street, Scarborough.

Silex Bya, off Flamborough Head, is frequently used by divers. A large car park is situated at the cliff top, the descent being made on foot. Depth is about 30 feet and visibility can reach 35 feet. The bottom is rock with plenty of crab, lobster, sea urchins, and plant life, but currents are dangerous when the tide is rising. Nearby North Landing is also a similar well-used site. Filey Brig, at the north end of Filey Bay, is noted as a spear-fishing area—if you do not hire a boat, expect a two-mile walk. The depth can reach 90 feet with visibility of 40 feet maximum. Farther south, there is Spurn Head, dubious diving but the site of the sunken town of Ravenser Odd. Air can be obtained from the Secretary, G. A. Wright, 46 Seafield Avenue, B.O.C.M. Village, Hull.

Little information is available on the stretch of coast from Hull to Southend and visibility is at its worst in this area. At Southend itself, dives off the pier can plumb 60 feet at high tide, but permission must be obtained from

the pier master, and visibility, at its best, will be around
12 feet. Air can be obtained by arrangement, from Mr. T.
Ludlow, 8a, Slaisbury Road, Leigh-on-Sea.

London can hardly be described as a diving area, but
so many excursions start from there that mention should
be made. It is here that Lillywhites of Piccadilly hold the
largest stocks of retail equipment in the United Kingdom.
Among the resident staff are Ron Chamberlain and Bob
Andrews, experienced divers who can supply advice and
sympathy in good measure. Lillywhites can also arrange
for the provision of compressed air. Air is also obtainable
most evenings, from A. Wicks, 8 Hatfield Road, W.4.
The coast from the Thames Estuary to Margate is
unimpressive, visibility being usually poor. However, the
site of the Roman Wreck of Pudding Pan Rock lies
waiting off Whitstable. The Whitstable Diving Company,
38, Oxford St. can supply boats by arrangement and air
in small quantities. The W.D.C. are also retailers of
underwater equipment, and manufacture wet suits.

From Margate to Dover, limited diving is available
just offshore, but here the presence of the Goodwin
Sands tends to produce poor visibility—and a lot of
wrecks.

PART FIVE—IRELAND

From the underwater swimmer's point of view Ireland—
North and South—is in a similar position to Scotland.
Scenery is majestic, the water is clear, currents can be
fierce and the sea rough, and it is relatively unexplored.
Thus information on sites is scarce. Around most of the
Irish coast it is advisable to dive from a boat. Boats are
reasonable to charter, except in the places that cater for

the line fishermen, as access from land is often difficult and this has produced a demand for sea transport.

Around Northern Ireland good diving has been obtained off Kilkeel, Newcastle, St. John's Point, and Ardglass. Dogfish, wrass, angler fish, and crab, have been reported as well as a large, but unsubstantiated wreck off the Point. A little farther north, near Capeltown, several cannons have been found, one of which now resides in Belfast. Good diving is also reported around The Maidens Lighthouse, near Larne.

The area between Dundalk Bay and Carlingford Lough is rated as interesting, with plenty of skate and dogfish and several wrecks.

In the extreme north, off Rathlin Island, marine life is reported as prolific, but the current is very strong. Air is available, by arrangement, from the British Oxygen Co., Castelreagh, Belfast, and also from Belfast Branch B.S-A.C. Contact the Secretary, Miss H. P. McGuire, at 104 Lansdowne Road, Belfast N.1.

Moving south, off Dublin, Lambay is a favourite diving site. It is here that the wreck of the *Tayleur* was discovered, and much crockery and many full bottles removed. This is not bad considering the *Tayleur* has been at the bottom of the sea for one hundred years. At nearby Donabate many of the salvaged remains are on display in a pub, The Brook.

Sligo Bay, in the north-west, is the site where at least two ancient ships foundered, the *San Juan di Sicilia* and the *San Pedro Major*.

The south-west is a veritable treasure trove. The wreck of the *Lusitania* lies eight miles distant off the Old Head of Kinsale, while the remains of the *City of Chicago* lies around the Head itself. Air and limited equipment can be obtained from P. Allen, Courtmacsherry Diving Services.

Several expeditions have tried to locate the wreck of the

E

treasure ship *Santa Maria* wrecked in Blasket Sound.
And the steam coaster *Agate*, wrecked in Kenmare River
in 1911, has just been located by Des Lavelle.

Valentia Island has everything for the underwater
swimmer. The Irish Spear-fishing Championships are
held here, because the visibility and marine life is so
good. Within Valentia Harbour you can enjoy sheltered
diving in 60 feet of clear water, and collect scallops. The
area is noted for huge pollack, skate and plaice. Wrecks
abound: the *Flint Castle* lies in 30 feet of water, the
Crompton in 60 feet, and search is going on for the *Mary
Brigitte*, a recent wreck of 1958 vintage. Air, accommodation, and equipment, can be obtained and boats
hired, from the resident Sub-Aqua Services, Valentia
Island, Co. Kerry (Telephone: Valentia 24).

Galway Bay has many wrecks in its vice-like grip, and
there are furtive tales of gold, but none has been located.
Air is available from Mr. J. Kennedy, Sacre Coeur
House, Athenry, Co. Galway.

PART SIX—HOLIDAYS ABROAD

Spear-fishermen can travel light, but the aqualung diver
needs equipment that is heavy to transport, and the
facility of an air compressor nearby. Fortunately, sites
that supply air are springing up everywhere. This still
poses a problem, as equipment is bulky and heavy, and
uneconomic to transport—especially by plane. The
answer is to stay at one of the centres that can supply all
the diver's needs. When preparing for a 'package' diving
holiday, bring along your own fins, mask and snorkel.
You may want to swim at places where there are no
facilities, and besides, one may, in a busy period, get

stuck for the day with fins that are too large, or small. One item that is sometimes not supplied is a life-jacket, and as this does not occupy too much space, pack this also.

The Zodiac Water Ski and Diving School is located on the Spanish coast at Calpe (Alicante). Accommodation is in villas on the beach, near the school. Beginners and experienced divers are attended by Rowena Barnes and Candido Jordano. Full particulars can be obtained from: Zodiac School, 1 Richmond Drive, Wolverhampton, England.

The Dolphin Club is in Spain, at Tamariu, on the Costa Brava. Dolphin have several years' experience in diving holidays. A full range of instruction can be given, and full details are available from: 23 Bedford Row, London W.1.

Visitors to Mallorca can be provided with a complete diving holiday through Pontinental, City Gate House, Finsbury Square, London E.C.2. Although aqualung diving is only obtainable at the Mallorca Pontinental village, snorkelling is provided at their other villages, at Ibiza and Sardinia. No doubt these last two will eventually also provide a complete diving service—possibly by the time this is in print.

At Malta, aqualung divers are fully catered for at the Mediterranean Aquatic Sports Centre, St. George's Bay, Malta G.C.—address your inquiry to M. J. Falla.

The latest in exotic diving holidays is provided at the unexplored island of Zembra, a few miles off the North African coast. The resident instructor/host is the extremely capable and experienced Reg Vallintine, and full details are available from: Neptune Watersports Club, 233 Strand, London W.C.2.

No doubt the largest in this field is the Club Méditerranée. Some thirteen holiday villages are located around the Mediterranean (actually one is in Tahiti). Snorkelling is available at all, and full aqualung facilities at: Cadaques, in Spain; Caprera, in Sardinia; Palinuro, in Italy; and Tahiti. Full information from: Travel Counsellors, 139 Kensington High Street, London W.8.

X. Photography Underwater

A photographic record of your activities is a rewarding and pleasurable possession in any sport or activity. This is particularly true of sub-aquatic fields, for the underwater world is a photographer's dream. Unexplored scenery opens up in every direction; sometimes the vista will be suggestive of a science fiction landscape, and some of its inhabitants just as bizarre. Spectacular rock formations, seaweed jungles, the delicate, translucent colours of the jelly fish, the eerie majesty of a long-forgotten wreck all cry out to be photographed.

Sub-aquatic photographic apparatus has evolved rapidly these past few years, owing to the impetus given by the inception of the aqualung. The field of underwater photography is open to anyone with the patience to acquire the technique. Of course it is not possible, in a single chapter, to cover fully a subject so vast and complicated as underwater photography; but a summary of basic essentials can be given that will guide the preliminary attempts of the underwater swimmer, and help cut down the proportion of failures.

Although photographic equipment has reached a far higher standard than that available a few years ago, some of the difficulties in underwater photography are insoluble at present, and will probably remain so. Visibility under water is comparable to that of a permanent fog on land. Sometimes vision can extend to 100 feet, and at other times be reduced to a few inches. Suspended matter, in the form of mud, silt, plankton, and other particles, causes this. There is no practical way of eliminating this 'fog'; thus it becomes necessary to adapt photographic technique to prevailing conditions. The same can be said of the absorbtion of colours by the water—but more of this anon.

The Evolution

The 1890's saw the birth of underwater photography. At this time several people, in different countries, were experimenting with the intention of obtaining photographs of the underwater world. The first to achieve success was Dr. Louis Boutan, a French biologist, who in 1893 obtained some fuzzy underwater stills. Boutan was not satisfied with these attempts, and continued experimenting with various cameras of his own design, surmounting problems never before undertaken, and culminating in the success of sharp photographs that have survived to this present day. The year 1900 saw the publication of Dr. Boutan's book *Progress in Undersea photography*, undoubtedly the first book on the subject.

As with all dedicated scientists, the primitive tools he had to work with impeded Boutan—but never defeated him. There was no high-speed 35 mm. film available. Boutan had to use clumsy, fragile glass plates, with wet collodion coatings that necessitated exposures in the region of fifteen minutes. The camera was housed in a large watertight metal box. Boutan also devised an ingenious method of artificial lighting for underwater use. A large glass jar, mounted on top of a barrel, enclosed a lighted spirit lamp, and by means of a tube the operator could spray magnesium powder over the flame. The barrel housed an air supply that ensured enough oxygen for a reasonable burning time.

About five years after the publication of Boutan's book

another Frenchman, E. Peau, built a metal camera housing, and started taking underwater photographs. Peau was working in murky waters, and devised a piece of equipment that enabled him to eliminate at least some of the dirty water between the camera lens and subject. A glass cone was filled with clean water and sealed at each end. Placed over the camera lens port, this cone extended the field of vision. It is still used for close-up work in dirt-suspended waters, such as examining defects in harbour and dam walls.

In 1913 J. E. Williamson invented a structure that brought him fame and fortune—the 'Williamson tube'. The tube itself was a simple enough device, consisting of a flexible shaft 3 or 4 feet in diameter, at the bottom end of which reposed a steel observation sphere. Through the glass ports of this sphere Williamson filmed the underwater world as the public had never before seen it —factually. Williamson made several highly successful underwater films, including the original 'Twenty thousand leagues under the sea'.

A Dr. W. H. Longley was probably the first to attempt underwater photography in colour. Longley developed his heavy brass underwater housing in 1917. A few years later, in 1923, he produced colour photographs of underwater scenery by natural light.

Approaching 1930, scientists were taking an interest in underwater photography in greater numbers: William Beebe with his famous bathysphere; Dr. C. H. Marvin; Dr. W. Schmitt; Sir Robert H. Davis—all made their contributions. About this time E. R. Fenimore Johnson started to manufacture underwater camera equipment. Today his Fenjohn Underwater Photo and Equipment Company is probably the largest of its kind in the world.

The year 1943 saw the inception of the Cousteau— Gagnan Aqualung. Although this apparatus was in no way photographic, it opened up a new freedom for the underwater swimmer and, more important, a potential market for underwater photographic equipment.

From here on the picture is more familiar. Cousteau produced *The Silent World* and many other films. Hans Hass has completed several books in addition to his films, and we even have regular series on television. Progress, considering the excellent start given by Dr. Boutan, was slow at first, but the latter years have seen great advances in this relatively new photographic field.

Choosing the Camera

The selection of the camera you intend to take under water depends upon a permutation of requirements: whether you desire still photographs or cine film; whether the equipment will be used for purely amateur purposes or with the intention of cashing in on possible commercial aspects; whether you want to concentrate on colour film or black-and-white and whether you need flash or other artificial lighting.

If we begin with the selection of a still camera, we come upon a further sub-division: standard cameras that are enclosed in waterproof housings, and underwater cameras that have watertight seals as an integral part of their manufacture. Let us first discuss the most popular standard cameras that can be quickly converted by placing them in an appropriate housing.

Starting with the elimination of cameras that for most practical purposes are too difficult to accommodate in an enclosure, we can cross off our list cameras with bellows, and cameras that utilise glass plates or sheet film. This guides us to cameras that are compact in design and use film in rolls. Desirable features would include: a minimum number of twelve exposures on each roll of film (you will not want to keep bobbing to the surface to re-load); an integral film-wind and shutter-cocking knob or lever (this eliminates one control shaft); and provision for interchanging lenses.

These items would seem to indicate a 35 mm. camera, and this type is, indeed, the most popular. The average interchangeable-lens 35 mm. camera is a compact instrument taking 36 exposures, and a waterproof housing can easily be made for it. Some models, such as the German 'Leica' and the Russian 'Zenith' and 'Leningrad', have housings on the market that have been specially made to take them.

Cameras with a larger negative format—taking twelve pictures 2¼ inches square on 120 film—would seem to suffer by comparison. The shape is larger, and costs, both initially and running, are considerably greater. But if the approach is purely professional, the larger negative can give better saleable quality—particularly with colour transparencies. Underwater photographs, however, due to their comparative rarity, do not suffer from this aspect to the same extent as those taken on land.

If economy of price is the main consideration, then a box camera in a simple housing can prove useful if its limitations are realised. The fixed shutter speed of a box camera, around 1/40th of a second, is adequate, but the small aperture, at about f/10, curtails exposure severely. This means that a reasonably fast film should be used for its wide exposure latitude—quality is not a prime consideration, or even attainable. Also, the fixed-focus lens will render anything nearer than 8 feet distinctly blurred, and the photographic visibility in British waters rarely exceeds this. It is necessary to fit the box camera with a supplementary or portrait lens that will fix the point of focus at 6 feet.

There are several cameras on the market that are designed for underwater use; that is with the waterproof housing of an integral part of the body. As only two, the Japanese 'Nikonos' and the French 'Calypso-phot', are currently available in Britain, and they are almost identical, we have space to run through a few of their features. Sealing is carried out by 'O' rings, with a glass port ensuring that water does not come into contact with the lens. Thirty-six exposures are available on 35 mm. film. Both cameras sport semi-wide angle lenses in an interchangeable lens mount; sadly, however, neither at the time of writing manufacture any other lenses. Let us hope that time will correct this. Range-finders are dispensed with—they are almost impossible to use underwater, focusing being carried out by scale. A range of accessories (close-up lenses, flash guns) are also available.

These cameras have other obvious applications, as they can be used on land without worrying about rain, or when water ski-ing or boating.

Selecting a cine camera poses similar problems. A decent length of film is needed to ensure a good run without re-loading. There is little one can do about the normal 8 mm. 'double run' film. This will run for 25 feet (2 minutes 5 seconds) and then the operator will have to surface and reverse the film for its second run. The Bolex H8 camera, however, will take a 100-foot spool of double run 8 mm. film, ensuring a run of 8 minutes 20 seconds before the operator has to surface.

16 mm. cameras take spools of either 50 or 100 feet—sometimes more. A model taking 100 feet is obviously better than the one taking less.

By virtue of the continuous movement, steady exposure is essential in cine. A coupled automatic exposure meter thus becomes almost a necessity—certainly a most desirable 'extra'. The same can be said of electric drive, for this eliminates the need for a winding control, apart from making long sequences possible. There are no underwater cine cameras available in Britain—if any are made at all. A waterproof housing has to be purchased, or made, to fit a standard camera.

8 mm. cameras are adequate for most amateur purposes. But if you fancy trying to make a profit from your filming, submitting to television, for instance, then you will have to use 16 mm. and a shutter speed of 24 frames per second as against the usual 16 f.p.s.

Choosing the Lens

Selecting the most suitable lens for the job in hand is just as important under water as it is above. Probably even more so, because on land it is a simple matter to change lenses if you are not satisfied with a specific focal length; whereas the underwater photographer is stuck with the lens he submerges with.

Of the greatest bearing on selection of a lens is the fact that particles suspended in the water form—in varying degrees—a floating barrier between lens and subject, reducing visibility and degrading the image. Added to this is the disadvantage that the lens, peering through its protective glass or plastic port, sees objects in the same way as the eye does when looking through the mask window: that is, everything seems nearer and larger. This has the effect of increasing the focal length of the lens (a standard lens used under water will function as a semi-telephoto). Now photographic visibility under water will rarely exceed 30 feet; in British waters it will usually average 5–7 feet of 'snappable' visibility. This means that the photographer has to utilise his limited area of vision to the utmost advantage by including the area visible to the left and right—a close-up-horizon technique—with a wide-angle lens. Thus it is obvious that the magnifying effect of water, turning a standard lens into a semi-telephoto, is a step in the wrong direction.

In addition to increasing the area of photographable visibility, a wide-angle lens enables the photographer to frame his subject from a closer position. This means

that there will be less water and suspended particles between the lens and subject, resulting in a sharper image.

Because all lenses suffer an apparent increase in focal
length when used underwater, a semi-wide angle really
becomes the equivalent of a standard lens; and it is
advisable, particularly in British waters, to employ a full
wide-angle lens. (Should cost prohibit this, a semi-wide
angle could prove adequate for most occasions.) Indeed, a
vast amount of good work has been produced with
standard lenses—particularly in the field of close-up. So
do not let the fact of a more suitable optic prevent you
taking your camera under water. The following table will
serve as a guide should your camera possess the facility
to fit lenses other than standard.

Camera	Standard Lens	Semi-Wide Angle	Full Wide Angle
Still 35 mm.	50 mm.	35 mm.	25–28 mm.
Still $2\frac{1}{4} \times 2\frac{1}{4}$	80 mm.	65 mm.	40–45 mm.
Cine 8 mm.	12·5 mm.	8–10 mm.	6·6 mm.
Cine 16 mm.	26 mm.	18 mm.	10–14 mm.

The maximum aperture (the light-gathering potential)
of a lens is an item that has to be related to cost. The
wider the aperture the more expensive the optic,
particularly in the wide-angle field. Although the ability
of the wide-aperture lens to produce results under poor
lighting conditions is an obvious advantage, the introduction of faster films—both colour and black-and-
white—renders this facility less useful. If money is
spent on additional optical equipment, it is better (in the
opinion of this humble writer) to lay greater stress
on wider angle than wider *aperture*. In general a wide-

angle lens with a maximum aperture of f/4 will prove adequate.

Housings

If an ordinary camera is to be used under water, it will be necessary to house it in a water-and pressure-proof enclosure. Only a few years ago the enthusiast had to build his own housing, but the growth of underwater swimming has been such that commercial housings for specific cameras, such as the Leica fitting Lewis Photo-Marine and the Russian enclosures for the Zenith and Leningrad, are available. In addition, specialist firms like Aquasnap will tailor a housing for almost any camera. In between the two extremes of do-it-yourself and purchasing a manufactured article, lies a third, hybrid, method: a clear plastic box of suitable dimensions can be supplied, complete with sealing lid, gasket, and control rods. This entails fitting the camera so that it is secure, and then drilling holes and fitting the control rods.

First, let us consider manufactured housings for specific cameras. Technical and Optical Equipment import an excellent range of Russian housings, which will fit the Zenith (a 35 mm. single-lens reflex), the Leningrad (a rapid-sequence 35 mm. model), and an 8 mm. cine. Built robustly of metal, they represent remarkable value.

Aquasnap supply a range of housings in clear plastic that will fit most still and cine cameras. The casings have infra-red welded joints, and can safely be taken down to 100 feet.

Aquafoto produce a cast alloy housing that will accommodate 35 mm. Kodak Retinette, Voightlander Vito, Agfa Optima, and 8 mm. cine Bell and Howell, and Eumig (supplied by Lillywhites).

The Aquascope—details from Sirocco—features a

quick method of camera removal, and can be ordered to fit a variety of still and cine cameras.

A thoroughbred in performance and, alas, in price is the Paillard–Bolex cine housing imported by Cinex. Designed for models H16 and H8, the construction is of metal with three controls: shutter release, lens aperture, and winding crank.

In the same quality class is the Rolleimarin imported by R. F. Hunter. Housing certain Rollei models, all the controls can be operated externally. It can safely be taken down to 300 feet, although the guarantee of safety at this depth applies to the housing, not the diver.

We have not the space here to detail the home construction of a housing, but we can mention a couple of firms that will supply the basic enclosure and a set of control rods for the do-it-yourself man. One has already been mentioned—Aquasnap; the other, supplying a sturdy tubular body in clear plastic, is the Aquasport. Details can be obtained from Lillywhites.

The selection, or construction, of an underwater camera housing depends, apart from the camera body, upon the focal length of the lens and the number of controls that are required. A housing that has an inadequate lens port or window can cause severe cut-off if a full wide-angle lens is used, while excessive controls need more holes drilled in the housing, creating additional areas of potential leakage and adding to the difficulty of construction.

The suitability of a wide-angle lens is a simple matter: just fit the lens and take a picture—you can check the negative for cut-off. More complex is the problem of which controls to dispense with. Some are obviously essential, but the order of importance between focus, shutter speed, and aperture causes vexed argument should one, or two, need to be omitted. If the aperture control were omitted, this would necessitate leaving the lens wide open to ensure that the shutter speeds could obtain the maximum variety of exposure. The consequent loss in depth of field and difficulty in focusing by scale makes this undesirable. Having (on paper at least) obtained aperture preference over shutter speed, we are left with aperture v. focus. From personal experience, the writer has found that if the focus control is omitted and the focusing scale pre-set, say at 6 feet, it is usually possible to swim into focus. However, if the aperture control is omitted, it is impossible to obtain correct exposure if the lighting changes. Here then is an arbitrary list of controls in their order of importance:

1. Shutter release
2. Film wind-on and shutter cock, or (in cine) motor wind
3. Aperture setting
4. Focus
5. Shutter speed

Of course some cameras do not have an integral film wind and shutter cocking knob, but this facility is true of the average.

The Film, Filters, and Development

The amateur underwater cine-photographer will rarely have the equipment to develop his own film, and will rely, for his results, on the correct filter-exposure combination. However, the still photographer is well advised to buy a daylight tank and do his own developing (of the negative, but not necessarily the print), particularly for black-and-white film. It is quite easy, just as cheap, and allows tremendous flexibility of the negative scale of tones.

There are various methods employed for black-and-white film. The most popular is to load the camera with slow or medium speed film, expose at double the rated speed (or even treble), and then develop the film for at least 50 per cent longer than the normal time. This has the effect of increasing the contrast, for underwater scenes are lacking in this respect. Although producing pictures that are probably better for publication, and that seem to be preferred by the average viewer, the result is not a correct interpretation of the scene viewed.

To obtain this, we have to use the technique of the land-based photographer when recording misty scenes. Like a surface mist or fog, the underwater world is composed of thousands of delicate half-tones; there are no rich blacks, although sparkling white highlights occur when, for instance, a shaft of light strikes ascending bubbles. Getting a full range of half-tones on print means using a fast film, normal exposure, and normal, or slightly less than normal, developing times. Alternatively you can use a medium speed film, over-expose slightly, and curtail development by about 10 per cent. The first method provides the widest tone variation, and the latter finer grain structure.

Before arriving at any of the mentioned methods, it is best to start your technique at the half-way mark, and to delve into modifications as you achieve confidence. For your first attempts, load your camera with medium speed black-and-white film (Plus-X, F.P.3), expose at a speed rated 50 per cent higher than that stated on the carton, and increase development 20 per cent. You can then adjust the combination if the final prints displease you.

Whether to use a filter with black-and-white film is another subject that is debated hotly. A light yellow filter can increase the contrast slightly, but the end result is a matter of personal taste, and you have to try both methods before arriving at any conclusion. A filter requires an increase in exposure, owing to the decrease in light transmission that it causes.

It is not intended to go into details about types of

colour film; but a few fundamentals should be explained
that are necessary if the colour photographer—cine or
still—is not to grope blindly, wasting both time and
money.

The most important aspect of underwater colour
photography is the fact that water has a filtering effect
upon colours at the red end of the spectrum. In practice
this means that red, orange, and yellow gradually disappear with increasing depth; at only 30 feet red has
vanished, and a little farther down the whole scene will
record a monotonous blue-grey. There are, however, two
ways of restoring the colour balance: artificial lighting
in the form of flash or continuous flood, will replace colours
to their surface intensity at any depth; but a still more
natural effect can be obtained by using a colour filter of
the appropriate density to correct the balance, although
this procedure is only effective down to a depth of 30 feet.
Suitable filters are manufactured by Kodak, and are
known as colour correcting red, or CC-R. They are
available in a range of densities, and the following table—
an unscientific one evolved by the writer from personal
experience—can be used as a guide.

Depth	Filter suggested	Increase in Exposure Required
5 feet	CC–10–R	30 per cent
10 feet	CC–30–R	80 per cent
20 feet	CC–50–R	150 per cent
30 feet	As dense as possible —try two CC–50–R	

Of course, one does not always swim on a level plane,
and it is difficult to change filters under water. If you
are stuck with the filter you fit on the surface, a good
all-rounder is the CC–40–R. One thing remains to be

pointed out: the increase of exposure suggested is purely arbitrary, and the colour correction, at best, will only be approximate.

Lighting and Exposure

For still photography, a flash-gun using expendable bulbs can, with modifications, be used under water—only the condenser, battery, and camera lead need insulating. The bulb socket can be in contact with the water, as an electrical circuit always takes the path of least resistance. The bulbs are fitted and removed in exactly the same way as on land.

The correct exposure calculations, when using flash bulbs under water, can only be arrived at by trial and error. Use the bulb manufacturer's guide numbers, and adjust the figure upon examining the results.

Flash-guns are manufactured to fit the Calypso-Phot and Nikonos amphibious cameras, and also the Photo-Marine housing. On the other hand, Aquasnap can supply a ready-made gun, or a kit of parts that you can construct yourself.

Cine photographers have a more acute problem: flash is out of the question, as cine film needs a continuous flood of light. Such equipment has to be adequately enclosed, with a powerful accumulator to compensate for the continuous drain on current, and prices are not cheap. An excellent lighting unit is the 300-watt Underwater Lantern, produced by Submarine Products. Using three 12-volt 100-watt tungsten iodine lamps in a triple reflector unit, it produces adequate lighting for cine purposes.

When using available or natural lighting, or a continuous flood unit, you will require the accuracy of an exposure meter. The Sekonic Marine is designed for the purpose of determining exposure underwater. A precision meter housed in a neat case that will withstand a pressure equivalent to 300 feet, the Sekonic Marine operates off a tiny battery. At least two firms—Lewis and Aquasnap—manufacture clear plastic housings that will accommodate a Weston exposure meter.

Exposure meters should be used in the most simple manner—from the camera position facing the subject. This method has proved successful in cameras that possess built-in, automatic exposure meters. Difficult scenes, such as back-lit subjects, can be handled after a little experience of average conditions has been obtained.

Items to Note

Underwater photography demands methodical habits. There are so many bits and pieces that can be forgotten, and the day ruined as a result; bags of silica gel to prevent internal misting of the housing; screws; tools; and spare 'O' rings. And all this is in addition to your aqualung equipment. Make a thorough list of every single item required, check it fully before you depart on a dive, and again before you leave for home.

XI. Underwater Science

PART ONE—ARCHAEOLOGY

The general area of sea-bed from the shore down to about 200 feet contains the greatest amount of archaeological and historical material. There are various reasons for this. Ancient ships, owing to a sparse knowledge of navigation, chose, wherever possible, the shipping routes that hugged the coastline. Many foundered on treacherous rocks that lay just below the surface, the coastline being a dangerous place for any vessel in bad weather. Also, the level of the sea does not remain constant; it has moved up and down—excluding tides—throughout the ages as the result of periods of glaciation. Over a period, the level of the sea has been rising, resulting in many towns, cities, and harbours of the past now lying many feet below the sea. Glaciation is not the only cause; land subsidence, earthquakes, and erosion have all contributed their share.

Thus the richest fields for exploration lie in the zone most accessible to the free-diver, and provided some training can be obtained, even a comparative layman is in a position to contribute to our knowledge of the past. In this respect, experienced divers in Britain are fortunate, for at Swanage, Dorset, what is possibly the world's first school in Nautical Archaeology has been established. Formed by the Institute of Archaeology in conjunction with the Scientific and Technical Group of the B.S-A.C., and presided over by Dr. John Waechter, a lecturer at the Institute, the courses consist of a series of week-end lectures and working dives.

The Scientific and Technical Group also have many projects in hand for those qualified to join. These include investigating the 'cranogs' (artificial islands) in Loch Lomond; a Roman well; a survey that has recovered many items of archaeological and historical interest from the Thames—for which the Group has received a certificate from the London Museum; and a search—so far unsuccessful—along the bottom of the Solent for the wreck of H.M.S. *Mary Rose*, a warship that overturned and sank in 1545.

The Roman Wreck at Pudding Pan Rock

Pudding Pan Rock is a shoal in the Thames estuary, about 4 miles North of Whitstable, Kent. The name derives from the large quantity of pottery that has, in the past, been dredged up by the nets of local fishermen. The first finds were, indeed, very suitable for cooking puddings—as the fishermen's wives were quick to note— although later, plates of various shapes and sizes, some plain and others with a simple embossed motif, were brought up.

The pottery is classed as 'Samian ware', and was made in central France in the second century A.D. The main production centre during this period was Lezoux, from where the pottery probably came, being transported by river to the coast of Gaul, and from there to London, a destination it never reached. But this is not strictly true, for the British Museum, in Great Russell Street, houses a collection from this very consignment. The ware is stamped with the maker's name *Satvrini*.

Several expeditions, both helmet and free-diving, have failed to locate what might be left of the wreck. Situated where it is, near the mouth of the Thames, care has to be taken with tides; and although visibility, given optimum conditions, might reach as far as 8 feet, it will more probably be in the region of 8 inches or less. Future expeditions will find the diving dull and uninspiring. There is even the point that there might never have been a wreck—there may have been some other reason for this accumulation of Samian ware. None the less, Pudding Pan Rock has, at the time of writing, the nearest likelihood of being the site of a Roman wreck in British coastal waters. For none have ever been found.

Lost Towns and Harbours

The story of Ravenser Odd illustrates one aspect of reclamation by the sea.

Spurn Head lies at the mouth of the River Humber, a curling headland in the shape of a crook, the side facing the river, and susceptible to silting up. At the beginning of the thirteenth century, marine deposits built up a small sandbank on the inside of Spurn Head. At first, local fishermen used the sandbank for laying out catches and equipment, but as the exposed land became apparently more stable, commerce moved in, and Ravenser Odd was born. At its peak, the town was a threat to its neighbour, Grimsby, and even had a Member of Parliament. Then the forces that had formed its foundation started to reverse the process; by the end of the fourteenth century, Ravenser Odd had disappeared.

The actual site of the town is still in dispute, but Ravenser Odd was—for a while—a very real place. Now it is covered by the waters of the Humber, or possibly the North Sea.

At 11 a.m. on the 7th June, 1692, Port Royal, Jamaica, was a thriving—albeit nefarious—town. By mid-day, an earthquake had reduced two-thirds of the town to below sea level. The death toll was two thousand.

Nearly two hundred and fifty years later, in 1959, the American, Edwin Link, led an underwater archaeological expedition that recovered a wealth of artefacts, and surveyed the remains of the sunken site, giving historians a wealth of material with which to reconstruct an important period of our past.

The list is endless. When the New World was first being explored, boats commuting to the Americas tended to follow routes dictated by the Atlantic currents. Historian-divers have charted these routes, and exploration has revealed the sites of many wrecks from this period.

In the Mediterranean, there are nearly sixty known submerged cities and harbours of the past. Among them are Helike, Apollonia, and the Great Harbour of Pharos. Fewer than a dozen have been surveyed by diving archeologists, and not one, at the time of writing, thoroughly.

Preservation of Iron and Wood

Technique and equipment has evolved to the stage where amateur diving groups are capable of lifting, and removing, comparatively heavy objects from the bottom of the sea. This leads to the danger of untutored enthusiasts removing artefacts without ensuring that the correct treatment for preservation of the objects is available. Iron and wood, after a long period in sea water, will disintegrate rapidly on exposure to air. However, there are occasions—such as difficulty in re-locating the site— when immediate removal might be advisable. For these occasions, the following notes might be of help. Many valuable finds are lost every year, due to incorrect treatment after recovery.

In the case of iron, the chemical treatment will necessitate removal of the oxygen that has formed at the surface of the metal. Marine deposits also form encrustations on the surface. These can be removed by gentle tapping with a hammer while the object is immersed in a bath or other water-filled container. If the iron is of a delicate nature like wrought iron, the removal is best left to an expert. It is of prime importance to ensure that the whole object is kept away from direct contact with air. If an adequate container is not available, the parts should be covered with wet material and further covered with plastic sheeting until a suitable receptacle is obtained. While immersed in water, the iron will keep indefinitely until an expert is consulted. Don't try to 'improvise' methods of drying: the correct process takes at least two months, and trying to shorten this time could lead to the loss of the item. Brass requires no treatment; just tap the growths off with a hammer and polish.

Wood, in fresh water, has an indefinite life, but in most sea waters it is susceptible to attack by shipworm. This organism can eliminate a sturdy wooden pile in a few short years. Some woods—probably by luck or certain oils present in their formation—will resist the ravage of shipworm for long periods, sometimes centuries, and our attempts at preservation are then directed towards removing the moisture in the wood without drying it—for this would cause its destruction—and replacing the moisture with paraffin (the wax, not the oil). The wood, having been kept immersed in water since recovery, is removed and placed in a suitable receptacle, which is then filled with alcohol until the wood is covered. A lid or covering is then placed over the whole assembly. This bath should last for four weeks, the alcohol being renewed every week. At the end of this period, the alcohol should be replaced by xylene and left for a week. The xylene is then renewed, and slivers of paraffin wax added until a well-saturated solution is obtained. Leave the wood in this solution for three weeks—a little longer will do no harm. When this treatment has been completed, the excess wax coating of the wood can be removed by polishing gently.

It must be pointed out that while this process can be used with complete safety on wood that has been rescued from fresh water, the results are not entirely predictable with wood that has been immersed in the sea. The reason for this, no doubt, is the presence of salt in sea water. Therefore, it is essential that sea-saturated wood be soaked in fresh water—with frequent changes—for as long a period as possible before commencing the alcohol bath.

The process can also be used to preserve leather or bone.

PART TWO—BIOLOGY

There are still vast areas of land that are biologically unsurveyed, even after centuries of exploration and scientific advance. Imagine, then, the problem that lies in researching a far larger area, the underwater world, from scratch, without the benefit of accumulated years of exploration. For many years to come, the trained free-diver will be of immense value to the scientists commencing to tackle this mammoth task (provided, of course, that in addition to his diving ability, he has had at least a basic course of instruction on the branch of science that he is assisting). In the field of marine biology, the Department of Extra-Mural Studies at London University runs, at the time of writing, a course on this subject for the comparative layman. It is to be hoped that education authorities will bring underwater sciences into the curriculum of many evening classes for the amateur, archaeologist/biologist free-diver.

It is not possible, in the space designated, to give even

a firm outline of underwater biology here. As in the
section on archaeology, a few examples followed by hints
on preservation and treatment will be given.

The Layman and Underwater Research

For several years now, the scientific group of the Westminster branch B.S-A.C. has conducted a botanical
exploration of some lakes in the Snowdon area of North
Wales. There are no botanists in the group; specimens
found are sent to Dr. Brian Seddon, National Museum
of Wales, for identification. By obtaining details such as
the maximum and minimum depths at which plants
grow, and their general distribution; temperatures at
intervals down to the bottom; type of bottom; visibility,
etc., the group are building up a set of data sheets that
will add to the natural history knowledge of these lakes,
in which so little exploration has been done. As the
identification of species is done by an expert, the divers
can get on with the aspect of underwater science in which
the enthusiastic layman can compete on level terms with
a professor—accurate recording.

Lakes, in any country, are rich in legend, and North
Wales is no exception. A 'sunken city' resides at the
bottom of Lake Bala, and a 'monster' at the bottom of
Lake Glaslyn—at the bottom because the monster was
killed before being 'deposited' in the freezing water.
Thus, while participating in the more tangible practice
of botanical exploration, every mound on the lake-bottom
is liable to titillate the imagination.

At sea, liaison between free-diver and scientist is
increasing. At the time of writing, at least five sub-aqua
clubs or branches are, or have been, collecting Mediterranean Gobies (the goby is an attractive little fish, one
species—*Mistichthys luzonensis*—of which can lay a
double claim to fame: it is the smallest known fish, and

also the smallest known vertebrate) for the University of Glasgow and the British Museum.

The Scientific and Technical Group publish a newsletter, in which requests for material by various museums are often published. Authorities concerned will give the keen diver every assistance regarding identification and details required. But don't, repeat don't, volunteer for work such as this unless you are sure that you possess the discipline to record with painstaking accuracy. Even failure can provide useful information; if a search for a specific fish or plant proves negative, its recorded absence could fit in a little part of the natural history jig-saw.

Collecting and Preservation

Collecting aquatic specimens, both flora and fauna, for the sake of a memento, is to be discouraged. For a record of your dive, a photograph is a far better medium. However, all free-divers should cultivate an active interest in underwater natural history. Fish *can* be interesting subjects (even outside a frying-pan) and this will often entail collecting specific specimens, and treating them for further study. It should be stressed that these preservation hints are for general use by the free-diver collecting on his own behalf; when collecting for an authority such as a museum, the exact preservation procedure for the particular item sought will be given. Specimens, even of a similar species, may require slightly different treatment according to the requirements of the museum.

Coral. A long soak (a week) in fresh water with frequent changes to remove the salt is all that is needed for corals. They can then be left to dry out slowly. Some corals, such as gorgonia, tend to lose their colour after exposure to light, and this can only be rectified by re-soaking in a dye of the same colour.

Fish. The animal should be alive for the best results. The

fish should first be doped, otherwise the muscles will
contract on fixing, and this is achieved by placing it in
fresh water for a few hours (for fresh water fish, use
distilled water). When you can pick the animal up without protest, it should be ready. It can then be killed by
dropping into a solution of 70 per cent ethyl alcohol and
30 per cent water. The body is then injected with a
10 per cent formalin solution, and preserved in the same
liquid. In the case of marine fish, make up the 10 per cent
formalin solution with sea water. Formalin can be obtained from the chemist, and the 10 per cent solution is
made up by mixing one part of formalin with nine parts
water.

Plants. Two methods are offered for preserving seaweed,
the one chosen depending upon your patience. The
second method is the best for display. (1) Soak the plant
in fresh water for six hours, changing the water at least
once. Drain off thoroughly, and soak in glycerine for at
least eighteen hours. Drain again, lay the plant on a good
quality unglazed paper, and dry in a dry atmosphere.
(2) Collect and keep the plants in sea water until ready
for treatment. When ready, drain the plant and arrange
on a sheet of good quality unglazed paper. Place paper
and plant on a sheet of absorbent paper and cover with
washed butter-muslin; on top of the muslin place another
sheet of absorbent paper. This procedure can be repeated
until a pile of plants interspaced with drying paper is
obtained. The pile is placed between two sheets of hard-
board, and gentle pressure applied. The absorbent papers
should be changed every day for three days; the specimens should be ready after seven or eight days. When
dry, the muslin should be peeled off carefully, when
the plant should adhere to the unglazed paper, ready for
display or observation. Where the plant does not stick to
the mounting paper, a touch of fixative might be needed.

Sea Urchins. If only the shell is needed, cut carefully

around the 'foot' and remove the innards with your finger. The urchin is then placed in a saucepan of water and brought to the boil. The spines can then be scraped off easily—but be careful, for the shell is delicate. A few drops of household bleach added to the boiling water will render the final colours more vivid. If the specimen is required with spines intact, remove the innards as before, wash out well in cold water, and dry thoroughly in a gentle oven with the door open. Most people find the smell of sea-urchin drying rather disagreeable.

Starfish. Starfish should be doped in fresh water as for fish. After several hour's immersion, it can be fixed for a week in a 10 per cent formalin solution. On removal from the solution, the starfish is tied down and thoroughly dried. If not tied down while drying, the starfish will tend to curl up.

XII. Spear-fishing

The pros and cons of spear-fishing have given cause to more argument than any other water sport. Nevertheless, its popularity is rising steadily. Possibly, in time, the camera will replace the spear—as it has the rifle on land to a large extent—although photography under water is much more difficult than on land, and the cheapest underwater photographic apparatus is far more expensive than its spear-fishing counterpart, the hand spear.

It has been suggested that this method of fishing is denuding British waters of its fish life, even though anglers, by sheer weight of numbers, probably extract a greater total of fish from the sea in a day than spear-fishermen do in a week. And there has never been any intimation that the rod and reel would deplete our waters.

Spear-fishing correctly practised is carried out using fins, mask, snorkel, spear or harpoon, and a deep breath. Aqualung apparatus is frowned upon as unsporting, and indeed has been rendered illegal in some countries.

Men have, for hundreds of years, utilised a spear or like instrument for the purpose of catching fish. But it is only since the advent of the mask and fins, giving man visibility and propulsion under water, that he has competed against the fish on more favourable terms. Even so, the most pro-spear-fishing diehard would agree that to spear a friendly, inedible fish is more than just unsporting—it is wanton destruction. It is therefore important to be able to recognise not only those fish most suitable for the pot, but also the inedible variety, whose death would benefit nobody.

Equipment

Essential equipment for spear-fishing consists of fins, mask, and spear; but of almost equal necessity is a snorkel, and some form of protective clothing. The last-named will include a weight belt to correct buoyancy, and a life-jacket for safety's sake. A knife might seem an extravagance, but considering the amount of tough line that the spear-fisherman could get entangled with, it could be considered essential. The only item of equipment not mentioned elsewhere is the spear, or harpoon, so let us dwell for a while on the various types and their capabilities.

The simplest underwater hunting implement, and one requiring a great deal of patience and knowledge, is the hand spear. This is a shaft of varying length, manufactured from wood, metal, or fibreglass, with a sharp steel spearhead, usually interchangeable. The velocity, or thrust, of the hand spear is often improved by the addition of a loop of elastic on the end opposite the head, turning it, in effect, into a hand sling spear.

When hunting with a hand spear, patience is required because of its limited range. Above average knowledge of the underwater world is required when fish have to be approached closely, and some fish, such as the poisonous weever, the sting-ray, and the cantankerous conger, are best avoided.

Despite—or perhaps because of—the above comments, many skilled spear-fishermen insist that hunting with the hand spear gives the most equal sporting conditions in man's contest with the fish. Certainly, many fish weighing over fifty pounds have been recorded as caught with this primitive instrument—ample proof of the degree of skill that can be attained.

Hand spears have been produced with a length exceeding 10 feet. But it should be remembered that in British waters, hunting often takes place in visibility of only 6 feet or less, and it is rather pointless looking for prey when you can't even see the end of your spear. A good all-round length for a hand spear in British waters is 4 feet.

Most underwater hunting is carried out with a spear gun. This instrument can be divided into three types according to the method of propelling the harpoon: rubber strands, coil springs, and compressed air.

The most popular spear gun is the type powered by rubber strands. This works on the same principle as that of the catapult or ancient cross-bow, though some models increase the power by adding a further elastic strand.

Although powerful, rubber-powered guns are the cheapest to buy, owing to the simplicity of construction. The price, no doubt, accounts for much of their popularity, while their very simplicity renders them less liable to mechanical failure—and easier to repair when they do fail. They are also usually the easiest of the three types of gun to load.

Of possible danger to the operator, as with a catapult, is a strand snapping while under stress or being cocked. Spare rubber strands are relatively inexpensive, but those in use should be checked regularly for faults or wear. Even if nothing suspicious is seen, it is a good plan to replace the strands at regular intervals.

The next gun, in order of popularity and price, is that utilising a coil spring as the power source. Coil spring guns are of more robust construction than their rubber strand cousins, the increased difficulty of manufacture being reflected in the price. This type of gun presents a more streamlined appearance than the rubber powered model, and the position of the handle in the middle of the barrel gives a better balance.

Coil springs lose their efficiency and power with use, and can even break, but this presents no danger to the operator. They can usually be replaced with ease. Ensure that no sand gets into the spring or any other moving parts, and also that you oil the metal mechanisms before and after use.

The 'Big Daddy' of the underwater gun world is the compressed-air gun, which is immensely powerful and easy to load. Air is pumped into a chamber and retained by a piston inside the barrel, which prevents the compressed air from escaping, and the gun may be loaded and fired many times without further pumping. Charging pumps are usually included in the purchase price.

Compressed-air guns are virtually silent in operation under water. They are used by the majority of spear-fishermen in competition, and at the time of writing represent the ultimate in spear guns.

Should a harpoon not prove immediately fatal, or even miss its target altogether, it can easily be lost. All harpoons are secured to the gun with a length of nylon line. The line is fed out by a reel or clip attached to the gun, rendering the recovery of the harpoon a simple matter.

The barbed head of the harpoon should be interchangeable, because no particular head is suitable for all types of fish. It is unlikely that, on a general hunt, you would have the correct head fitted for the fish you meet; so should you be hunting for a specific fish, the right head should be fitted.

The trident head—this can have two prongs or more—is often the most suitable for flat fish, smaller fish, and most bottom fish. Usually trident prongs and barbs are fashioned from soft steel, which makes them easier to keep sharp and straighten should they bend.

F

Larger game fish require a heavier spearhead, which is usually a single point, with one or more pivoted levers that prevent the harpoon from being pulled out too easily.

While on the subject of spear guns, remember that this instrument is designed to kill, and even the smallest type is capable of killing a human being. So here are a few rules that should be adhered to—not just most of the time, but ALWAYS:

Never point a gun, loaded or unloaded, at anyone.

Never carry a loaded gun on land—a gun should always be loaded or unloaded in the water.

Never hunt in the vicinity of other people, whether bathers, divers, fishermen, or yachtsmen.

Never fire a gun towards the surface.

Always use the safety-catch, but never rely on it.

Never leave equipment—particularly harpoon heads—around on the beach.

Under water, never let your gun dangle, keep it held correctly.

Should someone accidentally get transfixed by a harpoon, remember that its job is to hold tight, so do not try to pull it out. Call for a doctor, or get the patient to one, as soon as possible.

There are various gun licence and firearms acts, and statutory regulations that could apply to spear guns. But as these were not designed with this weapon in mind, the situation is a little confused. Certainly applicable is the following portion of the Gun Licence Act of 1870: 'An air gun or any other kind of gun from which any shot, bullet or other kind of missile can be discharged'. A gun licence costs only 10/–, and could put you on the safe side. In any case, it is a good idea to consult your local police for a ruling.

Of immense value to a spear-fisherman, if no boat cover is available, is a good float with a form of keepnet attached. This can be fashioned quite cheaply by blowing up a car tyre inner tube, and using a rubber adhesive to glue netting, or cloth, over one open end. The float is used covered end down, and the receptacle provided can be used as a depository for catches, or equipment, while the tyre itself can support a spear-fisherman taking a breather. One point: a float of any kind will scud across the water at a nifty rate in a good breeze or current, and can vanish in no time. So ensure that the float or raft is fitted with a line attached to some form of bottom anchor, or sea anchor, according to depth.

Training

Once you have obtained your equipment you will, no doubt, desire to get under water and bag a big 'un. But wait. If a thing is worth doing, it's worth doing well. A little advance planning and training will make you more competent, insuring against some frustrating experiences when you finally get hunting.

Spear-fishing is an exhausting sport. When you sight your fish, you have to get down quickly to dispatch him. The spear-fisherman descends—and ascends—at a much faster rate than the aqualung diver: pressures change swiftly, and the ears have to be cleared with machine-gun rapidity, causing greater stresses on ears and sinuses. Also, the spear-fisherman hunts utilising his own lungs as his sole air supply. Thus it can be seen that the first training pre-requisite is to get in good physical trim. When in the pool, do plenty of lengths and practise a clean, splashless jack-knife dive. After all, the fish are more used to the water than you are, and you are training to get on more even terms.

The principles of swimming with fins, mask, and snorkel are laid out in Chapter II. While brushing up on this, also read (if you have not already done so) the physical and medical aspects in Chapter III, paying particular attention to Exhaustion, Ears and Sinus, and Anoxia. The last-named is probably the greatest spear-fishing hazard (apart from a short-sighted hunter without his safety-catch on) because of the amount of breath-holding required. Don't practise hyperventilation—before the dive, only a couple of light breaths are required—and on surfacing, recover fully before the next dive. When practising in the pool, do not fight to hold your breath while under water. The secret is to relax—try thinking about something else. But don't forget to recover fully after each dive, and do forget about trying to set up breath-holding records. Your job is to get down, spear your fish, and get up: if you want to spend time looking at the scenery, then use an aqualung.

The first few shots with your gun will soon show you that a little practice is required. If you have access to the sea, obtain a float and hang your practice target (a piece of weighted wood or similar material) from it with a ten foot length of line. In a swell or choppy water the float will ride up and down, making the target jump about. This motion is not usually present in still waters such as pools and lakes, but you can still get some practice in. This procedure can, of course, be reversed or inverted. The line is tied to a weight on the bottom, and the wooden target is not weighted, but be careful not to have the line too short, or you will stir up the mud on the bottom.

There are many good books on the subject of fish haunts and recognition. These are written mainly for the student and line fisherman, but most of the contents contain valuable reference material. On the subject of recognition, don't overlook the fishmonger's slab; sometimes the fish are arranged whole, with tickets displaying the name, and a lot can be learned browsing with a good reference book (but don't forget to buy some fish once in a while to stop the fishmonger from getting annoyed).

The Hunt

The first problem, of course, is where to fish. British waters support a great amount of fish life, but areas vary according to conditions and physical structure. Also, the wiser spear-fisherman, by virtue of experience or home work, knows his fish. It is of little use looking for conger along a sandy bottom—or flatfish among rocky terrain.

Usually an area will be pre-destined, by holidays or accessibility. In this case, the reference books—plus a little judicious inquiring among the locals—are needed.

The more prolific sites are often around irregularities of the sea-bed, such as rock formations, wrecks, reefs, and gullies. Dense plant life will also often be heavily inhabited.

A clumsy, threshing dive will frighten off most fish. This is why we have been practising a clean, splash-free, jack-knife dive. A clean dive will slide you under water with a minimum of disturbance. Some people prefer to submerge by raising the top of the body out of the water and dropping feet first, but in this method your eyes are taken off your quarry for a second, and in that time he could vanish.

If possible, dive from a position where the sun is behind you. When your fish is within range, manœuvre into a broadside position and aim for the area just behind the eyes. The belly area is too soft, and the backbone—should you approach from above—can be too tough, especially for a hand spear.

Should the harpoon impale the fish but not prove immediately fatal, don't let the poor creature struggle, wounded and possibly in pain. Grasp it firmly by the back and use your knife to sever the spinal cord just behind the head—unless, that is, the wounded victim is a conger, when he should be left strictly alone.

Fish are not easily caught—or even seen. The successful spear-fisherman does not rush things; he will search thoroughly every rock, every hole, and every crop of weed. Acute observation is even more necessary in the case of flatfish. They usually lie on a sandy bottom, and blend with their background so well that only a really close look will spot them.

There is one type of underwater animal that is neither speared nor knifed—the shellfish. Crabs and lobsters are caught by hand. Average or smaller specimens are held across the back, but larger specimens require two hands—each hand round the arm of a claw. Care is needed because the claws possess enormous strength, and could crush a finger. The Edible crab, strangely, is not the only edible crab! Spider crabs and swimming crabs also provide good eating. Legislation prohibits catching crabs less than $4\frac{1}{2}$ inches in breadth, and lobsters less than 9 inches in length, or either if in spawn. This can easily be checked by looking at the underside, when the 'berries' can be clearly seen.

Fish to Catch and Fish to Avoid

It would be pointless to attempt, in the limited space here, details of fish recognition. For this a good illustrated book is required. Fish have their own popularity list with spear-fishermen. So let us refer to some of the 'top twenty', and aspects of interest to the underwater hunter.

Bass. Deservedly a favourite, the bass is elusive, unpredictable, and makes delicious eating. Powerfully built, and of silvery colouring, this handsome underwater game fish has been recorded at nearly 20 pounds. Although widely distributed, bass are most plentiful along the shores of the English Channel—particularly the west. They come inshore to breed in June, departing for deeper water in October, and are often found in the brackish waters of estuaries. Their diet consists of almost anything that is available: fish, crustaceans, marine worms, etc.

Conger. Much sought after by some underwater hunters —and left strictly alone by others—the conger is a nasty creature. Its eating qualities vary, ranging from excellent to soft and flabby. A formidable adversary, sometimes reaching a length exceeding 6 feet and weighing over 80 pounds, the conger should be shot in the head or mouth. If the harpoon should transfix another part of the body, then stand aside, for all hell will be turned loose. Congers usually inhabit rocky terrain, harbour walls, piers, and wrecks. They need a hole of suitable size to strike from, and are rarely seen swimming freely.

Dogfish. The two species found most commonly in British waters, the lesser spotted dogfish and the greater spotted dogfish, are presented in your fish-and-chip shop as 'rock salmon'. Thus you can form your own opinion as to their edibility. A type of shark, the lesser dogfish can reach a length of 30 inches, and the greater dogfish a length of 5 feet. They are well distributed all round the coasts of Britain and Ireland. Tending to prefer rough, rocky ground, and usually swimming at, or near, the bottom, the dogfish will rarely be found in open water, or a bare, sandy sea-bed.

Monk fish. Often confused with the angler fish (the angler is another species which may end up in the fishmongers as 'rock salmon') the monk is an ugly fish. Generally considered poor eating, the middle, in fact, has a core of white meat that, when treated, is known in parts of the West Country as 'Brixham ham'. Its tough brown skin was at one time used extensively in place of leather for covering articles. The monk is quite common in distribution, and is rather partial to the brackish water of estuaries, where it will usually be found lying on the bottom. Although the deeper water specimens can attain a weight in excess of 60 pounds, a big one for the spear-fisherman will probably be in the region of 7 pounds.

Grey Mullet. A good-looking elegant fish, there are three varieties of grey mullet common to British waters—Thick-lipped, Thin-lipped, and Golden. They are all well-known for their edible qualities. The grey mullets are numerous around the southern coasts of Britain, generally arriving in early summer and departing in autumn. They can reach a weight of 10 pounds, although the average is probably nearer 3 pounds. Grey mullet can be found in estuaries—often several miles inland—harbours, around piers, and in shallow waters where they feed off a string-like weed. They move in to the coast with the flood tide, and move out with the ebb.

Pollack and Coal Fish. These two species—from a spear-fishing point of view—can be considered identical. Opinions vary as to their eating qualities. Although widely distributed, the pollack tends to populate southern and western coasts; coal fish the north and east. They can both attain a weight exceeding 20 pounds, while the average is around 3 pounds. As with grey mullet, pollack and coal fish tend to 'arrive' with high tide, and depart as it retreats.

Weevers. Both British species of weever—greater and lesser—are to be avoided. The weever has poison glands at the base of the dorsal fin, and the poison is injected by grooved spines. Some people tend to decry the weever as not dangerous, but deaths have been recorded as attributable to its sting, and it has been known for the joints of the fingers, or toes, to become permanently stiffened. The weever, rarely more than 5 inches long, lies dormant on the sea-bed, usually half-covered with sand. Its flesh is quite eatable, but . . .

Sharks. There are several varieties of shark that visit British waters. Due to their enormous size and efficient teeth, all should be considered dangerous. This excludes the basking shark, which lives entirely on plankton—but then, who is going to wait around for an identification? The sharks that do visit British waters (porbeagle, blue, thresher, six-gilled, tope, and mako) are most common along the extreme south-west coast, although they have been caught as far east as Kent. Mostly inhabiting deeper water, they are rarely seen in the shallower reaches.

Common Skate. A member of the ray family, the culinary virtues of the skate are too well-known to require further comment. Fairly wide in distribution, the deep-water skate can reach a weight of 200 pounds. In shallow water, a big one would be in the region of 30 pounds. Skate are bottom feeders, rarely rising into open water. They are usually easily seen by the spear-fisherman, reposing on a sandy or shingle bed. When capturing your skate, keep well clear of its tail. Although not as dangerous as its cousin the sting ray, the skate's tail can inflict a painful wound.

Flatfish. This heading includes a vast variety of fish varying in size and culinary fame: the supreme turbot, the popular plaice, sole, and brill. To the underwater hunter, they all have one thing in common: they are usually found reposing on the bottom. A sandy bed is favourite, although flatfish are sometimes found reclining on a muddy bottom, or level areas of rock. The smaller and medium sized 'flatties' can be taken quite adequately on a hand spear, a gun being necessary only on the big ones.

We could go on for ever—the beautiful, easy-to-shoot, but almost inedible wrasse; the poisonous, Portuguese man-o'-war jelly fish—but we have to end somewhere, and this, according to the dictates of space, is the point.

Appendix A
Decompression Sickness

BY

DR. WYNDHAM DAVIES, L.R.C.P., M.B., Ch.B., D.P.H., D.I.H., M.P.

Another important indirect effect of nitrogen has been well described over many years. It is popularly known as 'the bends', and has also been called 'the chokes', 'the staggers', and 'the niggles'. These terms describe its effects. It is caused by a return to atmospheric pressure after being at high pressure, or exposure to low pressure after normal atmospheric pressure, so it is a problem of flying as well as of diving. Strictly, it is an indirect effect of the ascent, but since its foundations are laid during the descent, it may well be considered at this stage.

As the pressure increases under water, air dissolves in the body fluids and in the tissues, particularly the fatty ones. At this stage, the body fluids can be likened to a still soda-water syphon. As the pressure is released on ascent, so the bubbles of gas appear. In the body, these bubbles block off blood vessels in the joints, to give the 'bends', when the diver is cramped up with pain, or 'niggles' when the pain is much less—a vague rheumaticky syndrome. In some cases all that is produced is an area of itching of the skin. Such effects may be delayed for some hours, or there may be a dramatic sudden collapse, with paralysis of the limbs, severe distressed breathing, or heart failure. Treatment by re-compression is needed urgently, particularly when the heart or central nervous system is affected.

Whilst many of the troubles produced may seem to be minor, responding, like rheumatism, to a hot bath, it is suspected that some of the effects may be lasting. Cases of severe osteoarthritis of the joints have occurred in relatively young men exposed to continual decompression hazards.

Prevention of the acute, or chronic, effects is threefold:

(i) Not exceeding safe limits.

(ii) When the safe limits are exceeded, the rate of change of pressure should be such that bubbles of gas do not form. Prevention requires study of diving tables which, however, do not guarantee complete freedom from accidents.

(iii) Selection of divers, choosing those who do not have a great deal of surplus fat, or do not have associated lung disease that may increase the chance of air bubbles in the blood stream.

The treatment of decompression sickness is a highly skilled matter, demanding specialist treatment and facilities. Proficient divers who exceed the safe limits will normally have expert medical attention available, and recompression facilities. In many parts of the world today, men may be found who have consistently ignored these safe limits for some years; some were crippled at an early age, and because of their high pay, heavy drinking and early death often went together. With amateur divers today, these risks are no longer justified and some authorities would set a normal maximum safety limit of 130 feet (40) metres, with the following provisos:

(i) That no longer than ten minutes is spent at this depth.

(ii) That no further dives are made within six hours.

(iii) That well-trained divers wishing to exceed these limits should have permission from a responsible

authority who has assured himself that the risks
are fully understood and that the correct pre-
cautions have been taken.

It was mentioned earlier that decompression effects
could also arise in the air. It should be noted that it is
especially dangerous to run close to the safe limits for
decompression effects under water, and then take off by
plane within six hours, since, if the plane is unpres-
surised, or only partly pressurised, decompression
sickness may occur in the aircraft. Airline pilots and
crews should be warned specially of this. The Flight
Safety Foundation reported the case of a pilot and co-
pilot incapacitated within four hours of diving to depths
of only 20 to 30 feet (6 to 9 metres).

Decompression Table for Ascent Without Stops

Depth feet	Maximum Time on bottom inc. descent. mins.	Approximate time for Ascent. mins.	
30	no limit	1	
40	120	2	
50	78	2	N.B. Rate of
60	55	3	ascent 25 ft.
70	43	3	per min.
80	35	4	Single dive only
90	30	4	in any 12-hour
100	25	4	period.
110	20	5	
120	18	5	
130	15	6	

Decompression Dive Planning Tables

Depth (Feet)	Total volume of atmospheric pressure, air required for the dive (Cu. ft.)	Endurance of one cu. ft. of atmospheric air consumed at ambient pressure (Mins.)	Air consumption at atmospheric pressure (Cu. ft. per min.)	Water pressure — Atmospheres	Water pressure — Lbs. per square inch	Total time for dive (Mins.)	Total decompression time, i.e. time for ascent (Mins.)	Sum of decompression stops (Mins.)	Decompression stops in minutes — 10 ft.	20 ft.	30 ft.	40 ft.	50 ft.	60 ft.	70 ft.	80 ft.	90 ft.	Duration from surface to start of ascent (Mins.)	Depth (Feet)
0	a	1·00	1·00		0	a+1	0	0	0									a	0
10	1·30 (β+1)	0·767	1·30	0·30	4·45	β+1	1	0	0									β	10
20	1·61 (γ+1)	0·623	1·61	0·61	8·91	γ+1	1	0	0									γ	20
30	1·91 (δ+1)	0·524	1·91	0·91	13·26	δ+2	2	0	0									δ	30
40	270	0·452	2·21	1·21	17·82	122	2	0	0									120	40
40	404	0·452	2·21	1·21	17·82	184	4	2	2									180	40
40	539	0·452	2·21	1·21	17·82	246	6	4	4									240	40
40	674	0·452	2·21	1·21	17·82	308	8	6	6									300	40
50	202	0·398	2·52	1·52	22·27	80	2	0	0									78	50
50	311	0·398	2·52	1·52	22·27	125	5	2	2									120	50
50	391	0·398	2·52	1·52	22·27	158	8	5	5									150	50
50	497	0·398	2·52	1·52	22·27	202	12	9	9									190	50
50	778	0·398	2·52	1·52	22·27	315	15	12	12									300	50
60	164	0·355	2·82	1·82	26·73	58	3	0	0									55	60
60	221	0·355	2·82	1·82	26·73	80	5	2	2									75	60
60	334	0·355	2·82	1·82	26·73	126	16	13	13									110	60
60	459	0·355	2·82	1·82	26·73	174	24	20	15	5								150	60
60	548	0·355	2·82	1·82	26·73	207	27	23	16	7								180	60
60	637	0·355	2·82	1·82	26·73	240	30	26	18	8								210	60

70	144	0·320	3·12	2·12	31·18	46	3	0	0				43	70
70	203	0·320	3·12	2·12	31·18	68	8	4	4				60	70
70	262	0·320	3·12	2·12	31·18	92	17	13	13				75	70
70	317	0·320	3·12	2·12	31·18	114	24	20	16	4			90	70
70	425	0·320	3·12	2·12	31·18	153	33	29	21	13			120	70
70	533	0·320	3·12	2·12	31·18	193	42	39	32	18			150	70
70	646	0·320	3·12	2·12	31·18	237	57	53		21			180	70
80	134	0·292	3·42	2·42	35·64	39	4	0	0				35	80
80	190	0·292	3·42	2·42	35·64	60	10	6	6				50	80
80	283	0·292	3·42	2·42	35·64	97	27	22	16	6			70	80
80	408	0·292	3·42	2·42	35·64	141	41	36	26	20			100	80
80	476	0·292	3·42	2·42	35·64	168	53	48	29	22	2		115	80
80	609	0·292	3·42	2·42	35·64	212	62	57		28	9		150	80
90	127	0·268	3·73	2·73	40·09	34	4	0	0				30	90
90	188	0·268	3·73	2·73	40·09	55	10	6	6				45	90
90	273	0·268	3·73	2·73	40·09	90	30	25	14	9			60	90
90	341	0·268	3·73	2·73	40·09	112	37	32	21	18	6		95	90
90	445	0·268	3·73	2·73	40·09	151	56	50	29	27	8		130	90
90	599	0·268	3·73	2·73	40·09	201	71	65		27	17			90
100	117	0·248	4·03	3·03	44·55	29	4	0	0				25	100
100	194	0·248	4·03	3·03	44·55	57	17	12	12				40	100
100	307	0·248	4·03	3·03	44·55	99	39	34	21	18			60	100
100	388	0·248	4·03	3·03	44·55	128	53	48	24	27			75	100
100	443	0·248	4·03	3·03	44·55	146	61	55	48	28	6		85	100
100	470	0·248	4·03	3·03	44·55	155	65	59		27	8		90	100
100	640	0·248	4·03	3·03	44·55	219	99	93		28	17		120	100
110	108	0·231	4·33	3·33	49·00	25	5	0	0				20	110
110	186	0·231	4·33	3·33	49·00	52	17	12	12				35	110
110	321	0·231	4·33	3·33	49·00	104	49	43	21	22			55	110
110	461	0·231	4·33	3·33	49·00	159	78	78	37	27	14		75	110
110	633	0·231	4·33	3·33	49·00	215	110	103	50	29	22	2	105	110

Depth (Feet)	Total volume of atmospheric air required for the dive (Cu. ft.)	Endurance of one cu. ft. of atmospheric air consumed at ambient pressure (Mins.)	Air consumption at atmospheric pressure (Cu. ft. per min.)	Water pressure — Atmospheres	Water pressure — Lbs. per square inch	Total time for dive (Mins.)	Total decompression time, i.e. time for ascent (Mins.)	Sum of decompression stops (Mins.)	Decompression stops — 10 ft.	20 ft.	30 ft.	40 ft.	50 ft.	60 ft.	70 ft.	80 ft.	90 ft.	Duration from surface to start of ascent (Mins.)	Depth (Feet)
120	107	0·216	4·64	3·64	53·46	23	5	0	0									18	120
120	178	0·216	4·64	3·64	53·46	47	17	11	11									30	120
120	298	0·216	4·64	3·64	53·46	90	45	39	21	18	13							45	120
120	436	0·216	4·64	3·64	53·46	145	80	73	32	28	13							65	120
120	671	0·216	4·64	3·64	53·46	230	130	123	69	27	22	5						100	120
130	104	0·202	4·94	3·94	57·91	21	6	0	0									15	130
130	238	0·202	4·94	3·94	57·91	68	33	26	15	11								35	130
130	374	0·202	4·94	3·94	57·91	121	69	62	28	28	6							52	130
130	427	0·202	4·94	3·94	57·91	136	76	69	28	28	13							60	130
130	668	0·202	4·94	3·94	57·91	226	136	128	69	28	22	9						90	130
140	111	0·191	5·24	4·24	62·36	25	10	4	4									15	140
140	226	0·191	5·24	4·24	62·36	66	36	29	21	8								30	140
140	355	0·191	5·24	4·24	62·36	112	67	59	27	27	5							45	140
140	435	0·191	5·24	4·24	62·36	138	83	75	32	28	15							55	140
140	688	0·191	5·24	4·24	62·36	230	145	137	69	32	22	14						85	140
150	127	0·180	5·55	4·55	66·82	29	14	7	7									15	150
150	245	0·180	5·55	4·55	66·82	71	41	34	21	13								30	150
150	326	0·180	5·55	4·55	66·82	103	65	58	30	28								38	150
150	427	0·180	5·55	4·55	66·82	134	84	76	32	28	16							50	150
150	702	0·180	5·55	4·55	66·82	230	150	141	68	32	23	18						80	150
160	136	0·171	5·85	4·85	71·27	31	16	9	9									15	160
160	317	0·171	5·85	4·85	71·27	97	63	55	28	27								34	160
160	432	0·171	5·85	4·85	71·27	141	96	88	43	28	17							45	160
160	714	0·171	5·85	4·85	71·27	232	157	147	68	34	23	19	3					75	160

170	15									11	11	19	34	75·73	5·15	6·15	0·163	151	170
170	30								24	27	51	59	89	75·73	5·15	6·15	0·163	298	170
170	40							19	28	46	93	102	142	75·73	5·15	6·15	0·163	429	170
170	75					9	19	23	38	68	157	167	242	75·73	5·15	6·15	0·163	760	170
185	15									25	25	33	48	82·41	5·61	6·61	0·151	179	185
185	26								24	37	61	70	96	82·41	5·61	6·61	0·151	308	185
185	35							19	28	46	93	102	137	82·41	5·61	6·61	0·151	417	185
185	65				18	18	23	37	65	51	212	223	288	82·41	5·61	6·61	0·151	864	185
200	15									32	32	41	56	89·09	6·06	7·06	0·142	205	200
200	23								23	37	60	69	92	89·09	6·06	7·06	0·142	300	200
200	35							22	28	46	96	106	141	89·09	6·06	7·06	0·142	448	200
200	60			5	18	18	23	37	65	51	217	229	289	89·09	6·06	7·06	0·142	879	200
210	15									35	35	44	59	93·54	6·36	7·36	0·136	216	210
210	30						5	16	28	11	89	100	130	93·54	6·36	7·36	0·136	418	210
210	55			6	18	18	23	37	65	51	218	231	286	93·54	6·36	7·36	0·136	872	210
225	15								6	35	41	51	66	100·23	6·82	7·82	0·128	238	225
225	27						22	26	35	48	131	143	170	100·23	6·82	7·82	0·128	498	225
225	60			13	18	18	23	47	65	83	267	280	340	100·23	6·82	7·82	0·128	1,022	225
250	15								17	37	54	65	80	111·36	7·58	8·58	0·117	284	250
250	25					2	23	26	35	51	137	150	175	111·36	7·58	8·58	0·117	521	250
250	50		12	14	17	19	29	49	65	83	288	303	353	111·36	7·58	8·58	0·117	1,059	250
300	12								20	37	57	70	82	133·64	9·09	10·09	0·099	315	300
300	20					9	23	26	35	51	144	159	179	133·64	9·09	10·09	0·099	558	300
300	45	6	14	15	17	18	31	49	65	83	298	316	361	133·64	9·09	10·09	0·099	1,153	300

Note 1. Rate of ascent: 25 ft. per minute to first stop, thereafter 1 minute between stops and last stop to surface.
Note 2. Air consumption is based on assumed rate of one cubic foot per minute at ambient pressures.
Note 3. Ascent times: periods of 13 seconds and over have been rounded up to the minute above.
Note 4. Air required for dive: rounded to nearest cubic foot.
Note 5. Water pressures: 33 ft. of sea water is taken as 1 atmosphere 14·7 lb. per square inch is taken as 1 atmosphere.
Note 6. Figures in heavy type in the Duration column are optimum exposure times.

Appendix B
Diving Facts and Figures

One atmosphere equals a pressure of 14·7 lbs. per square inch.

Atmospheric air contains in volume: 78·05 per cent nitrogen; 21·00 per cent oxygen; 1·00 per cent argon; 0·03 to 0·3 per cent carbon dioxide; and minute traces of other rare gases.

The density of sea water varies according to its salt content, and this varies from place to place. Red Sea water is nearly 2 lbs. per cubic foot heavier than Baltic water.

The density of water varies with its temperature, and is greatest at 39 degrees Fahrenheit (4 degrees Centigrade).

An object immersed in water displaces its own volume of water. This reduces its weight by the amount which is equal to the weight of the water displaced. In effect, the weight of an object in water is the weight of the object in air minus the weight of the volume of water displaced by the object. Boyle's Law relates to gases, and states that 'For a constant temperature, the product of the pressure and the volume of any gas is always constant.' Thus when a mixture of gases is under pressure, each gas exerts a 'partial' pressure in proportion to its percentage in the mixture—if the pressure is doubled, the pressure of each constituent gas is also doubled.

1 fathom = 6 feet or 1·828 metres.

1 nautical mile = 6,080 feet or 1·853 kilometres.
1 knot = a speed of one nautical mile per hour.
Water depth (feet) to atmospheres—Divide by 33.
Water depth (metres) to atmospheres—Divide by 10.
1 cubic foot of salt water weighs 64 lbs.
1 cubic foot of fresh water weighs 62·5 lbs.

Appendix C
British Oxygen Co., Sources of Air

In addition to the cylinder charging facilities mentioned in Chapter IX, the British Oxygen Co. Ltd., has a network of depots that can supply medically pure air, by arrangement, in the following cities.

Northern Region

Belfast. Prince Regent Road, Castelreagh, Belfast.
Dundee. Ballindean Road, Douglas and Angus.
Leith. Seafield Road, Leith, Edinburgh 6.
Polmadie. 491 Aikenhead Road, Polmadie, Glasgow S.2.

Southern Region

Brentford. Great West Road, Brentford, Middlesex.
Bristol. Whitby Road, Brislington, Bristol 4.
Plymouth. Maxwell Road, Prince Rock, Plymouth.
Southampton. Millbrook, Southampton.
Wembley. East Lane, North Wembley, Middlesex.

Eastern Region

Brinsworth. Bawtry Road, Brinsworth, Rotherham.
Chester-le-Street. Vigo Lane, Chester-le-Street, Co. Durham.
Corby. Welby Road, Corby, Northamptonshire.
Leeds. Geldered Road, Leeds 12.

Western Region

Bromborough. New Ferry, near Birkenhead.

Cardiff. Maes-y-Coed Road, Whitchurch, Cardiff.
Wolverhampton. Lower Walsall Street, Wolverhampton.
Worsley. Priestly Road, Worsley, Walkden, Manchester.

Irish Republic

Dublin. Industrial Gases Ltd., 111 Pearse Street, Dublin.

Appendix D
Additional Reading

Although not exhaustive, the following lists contain books and magazines that the writer has found informative and entertaining.

Books

Technique :
B.S-A.C. Diving Manual
Diving Officer's Handbook, edited by G. Brookes (B.S-A.C.)
Deep Diving and Submarine Operations, parts 1 and 2, Sir Robert H. Davis (St. Catherines Press)
Spearfishing in Britain, K. McDonald and P. Smith (Stanley Paul)
Teach Yourself Swimming, F. Waterman (E.U.P.)
Illustrated Handbook of Life Saving Instruction (The Royal Life Saving Society)

General :
The Seas, Russell and Yonge (Warne)
Oceans, editor G. E. R. Deacon (Paul Hamlyn)
The Sea (Life Nature Library).
British Seaweeds, Carola I. Dickinson (Eyre and Spottis-woode)
The Fishes of the British Isles, J. Travis Jenkins (Warne)

Collins Pocket Guide to the Sea Shore, J. Barrett and C. M.
  Yonge (Collins)
Man Explores the Sea, James Dugan (Hamish Hamilton)
Creatures of the Sea, Capt. W. B. Gray (Muller)
Pond-life, W. Engelhardt (Burke)

Adventure:

The Silent World, J.-Y. Cousteau (Hamish Hamilton)
The Treasure of the Great Reef, A. C. Clarke (Arthur
  Barker)
Diving for Treasure, C. Blair (Arthur Barker)
2000 Fathoms Down, Houot and Willm (Hamish Hamil-
  ton and Hart-Davis)
The Frogmen, T. Waldron and J. Gleeson (Evans)
Captain Cousteau's Underwater Treasury, edited by
  J.-Y. Cousteau and J. Dugan (Hamish Hamilton)
The Reefs of Taprobane, A. C. Clarke (Arthur Barker)

Magazines

Great Britain:

'Triton' (Journal of the B.S.-A.C.). Eaton Publications,
  143 Fleet Street, London, E.C.4.
'Scottish Diver' (Journal of the S.S.A.C.). 1 Windmill
  Road, Hamilton, Scotland.
'Underwater World'. 2 Longfleet, Poole, Dorset.
United States:
'Skin Diver'. Petersen Publishing Co., 5959 Hollywood
  Blvd., Los Angeles 28, California.
'National Geographic.' National Geographic Society,
  Washington D.C. (Although this magazine does not
  always contain articles of underwater interest, when
  they do appear the result is superlative.)

New Zealand:

'Dive.' Wade Doak, Monowai Street, Wellsford, Northland, New Zealand.

South Africa:

'Fin Diver.' Box 33, Snell Parade, Durban, Natal, South Africa.

Italy:

'Mondo Sommerso.' Messaggerie Internazionale, Via Visconti di Modrone, 1, Milano.

France:

'L'Aventure Sous-marine.' 10, Rue de la Bourse, Paris 1er, France.

Holland:

'De Sportduiker.' P.O. Box 1341. Amsterdam.

Appendix E
Addresses of Use

The Confédération Mondiale des Activités Subaquatiques, or C.M.A.S., evolved at a congress in Monaco on January 11th, 1959, when delegates from fourteen national diving associations decided to found the World Underwater Federation. The number of member nations has at the time of writing swelled to thirty-eight. The C.M.A.S. is currently attempting to frame an international set of rules for diving. Divers journeying abroad would be well advised to contact the appropriate member country in advance if they have no diving knowledge of their destination. The administration offices are at 34, Rue du Colisée, Paris (8e) France. The following are a selection of affiliated bodies.

Australia: Underwater Skindiver's and Fishermen's Assn. of Australia, P.O. Box 56, Hampton, Victoria.

Belgium: Federation Belge de Recherches et D'Activités Sous-Marine, 5, avenue Jules Colle, Waterloo.

Canada: Vancouver Island Council of Divers, 4103, Borden Avenue, Victoria, B.C.

Finland: Suomen Ureilusukeltajain Liitto ry, P.O. Box 514, Helsinki.

France: Federation Française d'Etudes et de Sports Sous-Marine, 24, quai de Rive-Neuve, Marseille.

Great Britain: British Sub-Aqua Club, 25, Orchard Road, Kingston-on-Thames, Surrey.

Ireland : Irish Sub-Aqua Club, 127 Lower Baggot, Dublin.

Italy : Federazione Italiana delle Pesca Sportiva, Viale Tiziano, 70, Rome.

Russia : Fédération des Sports Subaquatiques, de l' U.R.S.S., B.P. 4710, Moscow D.362.

U.S.A. : Underwater Society of America, 721, St. David's Avenue, Warminster (Bucks Co.) Pennsylvania.

Although they are not directly affiliated to the World Federation, The Scottish Sub-Aqua Club are always ready to impart advice and knowledge to visiting divers. The Secretary is Frank Galloway, B.Sc., A.R.C.S.T., 38 Kinmount Avenue, Glasgow, S.4.

Index